I SURVIVED
and
SO WILL YOU

(Based on True Life Events)

Shawnetta Faust

Disclaimer

All erudition contained in this book is given for informational and educational purposes only. The author is not in any way accountable for any results or outcomes that emanate from using this material. Constructive attempts have been made to provide information that is both accurate and effective, but the author is not bound for the accuracy or use/misuse of this information.

First Printing: 2018
ISBN:9780692168608
(Address)

Dedication

I want to dedicate the book to my husband, Barkee Faust, for always being my biggest supporter in all I do. Thank you for your consistency every day. Thank you for loving me and the kids unconditionally and praying for us daily. I watch you pour, give, and sacrifice daily into everyone that crosses your path, often with no thank you or kudos in return. I want to publicly decree and declare that God is positioning you in the place of abundance. Your latter days will be greater than your former! Your children will rise up and call you blessed. God is elevating you, creating a platform that provides you with unlimited options. I decree this in Jesus name.

To my amazing children: Agnes, Samadiya, Shaniyah, Ashantae and Jaliyah whom I love dearly. I thank God for you all each day. You have made me stronger, better and more fulfilled than I could have ever imagined. I love you to the moon and back. Continue to look to the hills where your help comes from. Your help comes from the Lord and shall always.

In Memory Of: My Grandmother Katie Mae Kennedy Wise and My Mother Andrena Denise Wise - Rest In Peace

Acknowledgement

First, I want to thank God for keeping me safe all through the years. I am grateful for His hand being on me daily. I thank you for being there for me when nobody else was. Thank you for being there to catch me when I fall.

I am grateful to everyone who has played a part in my life. If you prayed for/with me, thank you! If you had a positive word to lift me, thank you!

I would like to express my special thanks and gratitude to my husband and children for being my number one pushers. Thank you for your patience with me!

To my grandmother, Katie Mae, who is resting with Jesus, thank you for picking up where my mother left off and doing it with grace. Thank you for doing your best to raise me to be the woman I am today. I am forever grateful to you for the many tears, sacrifices and prayers you prayed for me. I love you always.

To my cousin, Barbara Ballard Belton, for always being a listening ear when I needed it, I recognize your relevance, thank you.

I say a big thank you to my God Mother, Crystal White, who picked up the pieces working two jobs to assist my grandmother with raising us even neglecting herself to make sure we had all we needed.

I appreciate my uncle, John Wise and Bruce Wise; thank you for the parts you both played in being the best uncles I could have asked for. Special thanks to my uncle, Goo who has been my ride or die uncle from day one.

To my friends, Betty Keitt and Bobbie Keitt, who have been like mothers to me, and whom I call my aunt (and nobody can tell me they are not my aunt), thank you for the many prayers, the home when I needed a place to lay my head as well as my children. Thank you for the continued support and motivation throughout the years to write my book. Thank you for pushing me. Even when I felt like the end was near, you both played a major part in my life and I appreciate you.

To my cousin, Lasundra Keitt, and best friend, thank you both for remaining my sister through it all and not judging me throughout the years. Thank you for being another constant motivator in my life and seeing the good in me in spite of what anyone said to counterclaim that.

Last but not least, thank you to my God-Father, Apostle Ryan McJimpsey, for being a praying God-Father and praying me through some of the worst times in my life. The love you and Erica have shown not just me, but my brothers as well – I cannot be thankful enough.

I love each and every one of you for the roles you played in my life and will forever be grateful.

Contents

CHAPTER ONE

There Was Something Missing...

From the age four, down to twelve, for any girl, life is supposed to carry the best of times when she gets to enjoy the happiness that a family - a complete one - has to offer. At age four, her first basic instinct is to probably know what it means to be human since by then she has begun to talk clearly, to walk briskly, and to feed herself without anyone's help. At this age, she begins to feel human already, to understand the world as it is and to recognize her place in it. Undoubtedly, this should be a time in her life when she hardly has anything to worry about.

That wasn't my childhood!

Maybe it was, but in a most twisted and warped manner. As far as I remember, all I could feel as I looked down at my mom that day was the joy of her having so many flowers surround her, as well as so many people that loved her being around and wailing over the little box they put her in.

I didn't understand why they cried because I wondered, *Mom looks beautiful, she's sleeping, and better still, she has so many flowers around her. Why are they crying?* It didn't make much sense to me at that time. I only remember overhearing my grandmother and my aunt discussing a man that turned himself in to the police for killing her. I didn't even understand that death meant I was never going to see my mom again. It was a pitiable situation any four-year-old shouldn't have to experience.

After the funeral, my grandmother, Kathryn, would cry morning, noon and night but I didn't understand why. The last thing any mother would

11

want is to see her child being laid to eternal rest while she's still alive. No feeling of hurt beats that, and it is only now after I have grown that I got to understand this better. I am sure the last thing my grandmother thought would happen to her at such a young age of about thirty-five years was to have five children. She already had three children, of which the eldest of them died horribly in the hands of her boyfriend. She was nineteen years old! This nineteen-year-old just left her with three extra kids to add to the remaining two she had. How exactly was she supposed to cope with raising five kids in a two-bedroom house? Even though she had the help of Mr. Rogers, her boyfriend at that time, it was just too much responsibility for them considering their social status.

She took me and my two siblings, Jody and Frank, who were three years old and one year old.

I was born in Columbia. After my mother's death, we ended up being raised in a neighborhood known as Pinehurst. To be fair, Pinehurst wasn't really a bad place to raise a kid but if the circumstances surrounding the growth of a four-year old girl does not warrant growing uprightly, with parents to care and guide while having the right set of people to mingle with, then, who is to blame if such a girl would later grow up to live a life that would be the exact opposite of what a decent girl should be?

My childhood was rough, a period which I had to experience so much than most average humans should. All these events that have led to where I am today were as a result of the choices and opportunities to that came during that period.

But I am still grateful that in the long run, I am able to tell all that had happened as a tale to encourage as many people that have or are passing through similar ordeals.

13

Shawnetta Faust

I am grateful that I am now in a position to boldly tell anyone who cares to listen that regardless of the choices they decide to make for themselves, regardless of whether it was up to them to make these choices or not, regardless of the unfortunate situations that life decides to throw at them, they can still come out victoriously with a changed life. They can still become all they have ever dreamed of becoming, and they can still ultimately live up to that expectation that the world around them recognizes as successful.

This is my rationale for wanting to share my story, and I believe that after you read my story to the last word, you should definitely not remain in the same head and mind space as you are right now at the beginning. At the end of this book, something must have changed within you, and it'll be up to you to cultivate this and grow it into a passion that would ultimately transform the reason for your existence into meaningful feats of fulfillment.

Well, let's get back to my story, shall we?

So, at the age of four, I would see my grandmother hurt almost every day by the loss of her daughter. Many times, I overheard her praying in her room, asking God for the strength to take care of us. Those days, I would stay behind the door, laughing at how she cried while praying. I didn't understand why she decided to cry out loud whenever she prayed. Although there were moments that, in a way I couldn't explain, I knew something hurt her badly and it tore her apart at that time. Now that I think about it, it must have hurt her more to lose my mom to a rather irritating circumstance. My mom was killed at the age of nineteen by her over-jealous boyfriend who didn't want her to leave him when she decided it was time to exit the toxic relationship.

15

All the five children – I and her two sons, together with my two brothers – shared a room. And being the only girl out of us all, sometimes, my grandmother made to sleep in her bed while she would sleep on the couch. She did this to get me away from the boys, and to give me more space as a little girl. It just wasn't the ideal environment to raise a young woman that was supposed to make a reasonable difference in life. You will understand why soon enough.

Apart from my grandmother, we were nothing but abandoned children. Apart from the fact that my father was a drug addict, thief and dealer, he also understood next to nothing what it entailed to care for his own child. The only responsibility he felt towards me was to pick me up once in maybe every five months just to drop me off at his sister's house on those weekends. On each of these few times, he was always high on drugs, and we got pulled over by the police many times. I hated going with him, but I had no choice.

His sister's place wasn't bad since I had her daughter, Anika, to play with. We were around the same age, but she was two years older than me. We would play all the girly plays together, but even though I was quite young, it started to feel like something was missing. My father's sister would braid my hair and try her best to take care of me whenever I was at her place, but somehow, it just couldn't replace the feeling of having my own mother around. I was too young to understand what I was feeling, but a large part of me knew something wasn't right. I just didn't like that fact that Anika had a mom, and I didn't anymore. I had my grandmother, but it didn't feel the same. I remember a few times I would pick up fights with Anika just, so she would call her mom, "mom."

But my grandmother played her part well, trying her best with the five of us. However, things were never the same for her as it used to in the beginning. She had to pick up a second job just to support us. I would see her wake up very early in the morning to prepare for her first job while trying to get us ready for school. The only other time I got to see her throughout the day was at night when we were already in bed, and she would come to kiss us goodnight. I remember that majority of the time, I feigned sleep and would hear her stand over by my bedside and prayed for me not to find a man like the one my mother had.

Time flew past fast, and it was already my 5th birthday. My grandmother tried all within her power and means to make it as special as possible. I can still vividly recall the cake and the ice-cream, all of us gathered at the dining table to celebrate with pink balloons hanging all around the room. In fact, my mom's best friend, Amy, was at my fifth birthday party, and she came with a lot of gifts. I had no idea who she was at that time, but I only noticed she came around more often after my mom was killed. I remember she was now helping my grandmother with a lot of gifts for us, especially at Christmas. Even though they had no idea that I knew, I saw her sneak in bikes and a lot of other wrapped gifts that year, talking to my grandma about how we were going to love what Santa brought. So, it was a really nice fifth birthday party, but I felt so empty without my mother.

It was hard to be the only girl in the house and to make it worst, I was never allowed to go outside to play with the other girls. My grandmother felt I would be wrongly influenced by peer pressure if she allowed me to play with other girls in the neighborhood. While she was at work, she would warn us never to go outside to play with the other kids. On my way from school, I would see the kids next door playing in the yard and wished so badly to join them. I just couldn't because my grandmother wasn't home, and Mr. Rogers wouldn't go outside to the yard after a hard day's job. So, our routine was pretty standard - we went to school, came home, did homework, and watched TV until it was time for bed.

Things went on this way until I was seven when my life began to take a downward spiral. It was when I started to understand things in my immediate surroundings better. Since my world centered around going to school and watching TV, and, as I thought then, not having my grandma around most of the time to teach me vital life lessons, I found myself learning from everything and anything I had the opportunity to learn from. One night, my grandmother accidentally forgot her cigarettes on the counter. I knew its uses. I had seen people smoking it several times on the TV. Seeing that those that smoked it looked pleased doing it so, the first instinct I had on sighting the pack of cigarettes was to smoke it. I took out a stick out of the pack and smoked it. I loved the way it tasted. A part of me knew that my grandmother was not going to validate such an act. Immediately I was through, I ensured that she never found out. Besides, she was never home anyway, so there was no way she would smell it.

My grandmother's boyfriend, Mr. Rogers, never came out of his room all day whenever he was back from work, so I started stealing his cigarettes, too. I would go into the bathroom and pretend to be taking a shower. There, without anyone knowing, I would take my time to smoke the ashes out of cigarettes. Whenever I was done, I would try to cover up the smell with my grandmother's perfume. Even if she'd perceived any smell of smoke, Mr. Rogers smoked too, so she had no reason to suspect that it was me

21

since the odor rested on almost all his clothes and in the house heavily.

But smoking was also not the only thing I saw on TV. People who smoked also drank liquor and I badly wanted to try that, too. My grandmother used to have card parties over the weekend with her best friends, and there was usually plenty of alcohol. I knew my grandmother didn't drink, but Mr. Rogers did, and so did their friends too. This was why they always had alcohol over at the house to party. One day, I decided it was time to try out what I had seen. I stealthily ducked behind a chair, and immediately they all stood up to dance, I poured myself a little Hennessy into a cup and snuck back into my room. There was a sense of fulfillment I felt as I now had alcohol like the mature women on the TV and I could also smoke a cigarette. While they danced the night away in the living room, I drank and smoked my life away in the bathroom. My grandmother never noticed anything even after that night, and then it became a habit for me. The only thing she knew was that Mr. Rogers's liquor and her cigarettes reduced each day, but it was easy to conclude that her boyfriend was the one doing himself the honors.

I was a kid, but all I knew was that there was a void that needed filling. And this is usually the origin of the majority of the addictions most of us get used to. There's usually a sizeable unfilled space within, and we would typically jump at the next thing that seems to be the best solution to filling it. Of course, the bad habit we take on never gets to fill this void permanently; it's only a temporary feeling of fulfillment that tends to take all our problems away until we're in our right frame of minds again to face the harsh reality of the situation we find ourselves.

Even my dad never noticed I had picked up a life-damaging habit at such a tender age. I remember there was a weekend he came to pick me up and I was so drunk that I didn't understand or remember a word of what he was saying to me. He was too stoned as well to even notice how wasted his poor daughter was. He dropped me off with his sister as usual, and I remember wetting the bed that night. I knew it was the alcohol.

My life continued that way, and I knew that whatever it was I was missing, the cigarettes and alcohol shifted my mind from thinking about it. It felt like I was happy now and I had nothing to worry about anymore.

It might have been better if I was alone in my twisted world. I feel bad to have dragged my brothers down this road. I didn't know any better to prevent them from following in my footsteps; I was quite young myself. Jody, my immediate younger brother, was just a year younger than me. In fact, his birthday is a day before mine, and we usually joked about how we are the same age

24

for one day. He was definitely old enough at that time to notice all I was doing, and he wanted to try the same thing, too. Although I was the oldest sibling, he had no one else to attach himself to or advise him otherwise. His dad never came around to see nor care for him. My youngest brother, Frank, never got to see his dad either and I was the only one they could look up to. I was a bad sister.

My grandma was actually trying her best the best way she knew how to. She was working two jobs and with the help of my mother's best friend, Amy, tried to raise us well enough. However, it didn't feel like a complete package to me, and I had to choose a path for myself that filled the void of not having my mother around.

From stealing cigarette and bottles of Hennessy, I had already begun writing a chapter of my life that would take several years to be completed.

CHAPTER TWO

Taking My Grandmother Through Hell

I have learnt that life is a progression – a string of events that often start with a single action which leads to the next and then to the next before the final consequence which might be negative or positive.

Whenever I remember my past, I like to think that that single act of drinking or smoking I exercised from my childhood was the first of many acts that led me down the ruinous path, where I eventually regretted a lot of things.

Many young people sometimes lose focus in life. They let their curiosity or, better still, naiveté to get the best of them and before they know it, they are already doing a lot of things they shouldn't be doing. I was there. And I regretted some of the actions that I took back then. But there was no stopping then.

After smoking and drinking for the first time, I kept doing them. I felt no need of stopping. I felt that they liberated me from the incompleteness that I had and before I knew it, the urge to do them had worsen.

Something that I had initially seen on television became a strategy for me to cope with being motherless and for being in a new environment. I was living the life in the television and I didn't mind.

And I had no friends at all! Children naturally didn't like me, and I thought that I didn't need them. I thought that I had a mind filled with worries that they might never understand. As time went on, and as I continued to live like a recluse except when I played with my brothers, I realized that whenever I got into trouble or whenever I was frustrated, I would sneak more cigarettes or liquor and spend hours getting them into my system. I downed as many cups as I could, and I also smoked enthusiastically, loving the way the smoke puffed out of my lips to briefly become foggy in front of me.

I was eight years old then but, in my head, I was twenty-one. And I began to act like it. It was around this period that men became attractive to me. It didn't surprise me that those that easily attracted me are older – far older men. I would see them in the neighborhood and I would stare at their handsome features, at their thick legs or at their glinting beards, all the time finding it amusing that I admired them. These men included my teachers in school.

It went on like this – my new-found sport of admiring men from a distance – but by the time I was twelve years old, things took a turn for the worse. My grandmother began to allow me to go outside and we just had to be back in by the time the street lights came on.

"You don't come into my house before the lights come on." She would say, "I trained y'all properly right."

If only she knew those words meant little to us!

If only she knew that at that age, I had begun to submit myself to just anything that caught my attention. While my little brothers found friends, wanted to play basketball and do "boy's things", I wanted to find things that excited me. I wanted, by all means, to please myself with everything that I did. Besides, how many twelve-year-old children have access to liquor and are a-full-pack-a-day cigarette smokers?

Pleasure is something that I have found to easily distract or mar us as we grow. Finding pleasurable things such as cigarettes or alcohol make us think we are better than others, that we are happier than they are, or that we are better off without them. It limits our interaction with people and our personal growth, for the better. It is opium – an almost irresistible urge that suddenly takes over and makes us do things that would only harm us more.

It was while my admiration for older men was gradually reaching its peak that Uncle Freddie came to stay with us. He is my grandmother's brother and was going through a divorce with his wife at the time. He desperately needed a place to stay. My grandmother, ever the benevolent woman, allowed him to stay with us. This indirectly contributed to making my life more fun and destructive than it already was.

Even though he was such a cool person, Uncle Freddie smoked marijuana a lot; and that wasn't so cool a thing to do, especially when there's a little girl around, watching. I would see him smoking his joints in the backyard and boldly tell him that I wanted to try it. Surprisingly, he never muttered a word about this to my grandma. Instead, he smiled cheerfully, offered me his roll of Marijuana and watched; he fascinated by the way I dragged on it with a lot of joy in my heart.

Marijuana is obviously different from the cigarettes that I was used to, and I had to inhale it first in order to know. I felt on top of the word. When people spoke to me, it sounded funny to me. When I glanced around me, it felt like the walls or the open fields were moving spirals, entertaining me with their funny looks and slow twirling. Everything, moving and unmoving, was alive!

Uncle Freddie was more like the carefree uncle who would let you get away with murder if you told him you killed someone, so he often offered me more rolls. I often took them gladly. I would puff the smoke to his face and he would laugh heartily. No one knew this, and the secrecy of our act bonded us.

With Uncle Freddie in our house, I had access to more items of pleasure and this wasn't just cigarettes, Marijuana or alcohol anymore. They included hard drugs since Uncle Freddie worked a full-time job and often blew all his money on them. We would stay up late, getting high and laughing at everyone else in the house. Sometimes, we would stare at each other and laugh for no good reason. To me, he felt like the perfect crime partner and now, I wonder what if it had been the same to him too. I only knew I felt so happy then, nothing else mattered but abusing those drugs.

Uncle Freddie also fixed cars part-time on the side of my grandmother's house. There were always men and women who came to get their cars fixed and I got to see some fine men during the process. The women who came to the shop were more than the men, I think, but I never really paid attention to them.

There was a man among the many customers who seemed to have a different problem with his car every week. I noticed he would stare at me and I would stare right back at him, blushing, amused by the attention that such a grown –up man was giving me, the way his eyes would linger for long on my shoulders and at my chest. I have caught him staring at my legs as if he admired them dearly. I felt grown-up.

One day, while my uncle headed to a store to get the part for the man's car, he left him at the house. I cannot remember who it was that approached the other first, but I remember that we exchanged words and for the first time. It was the first time I heard a man refer to me as "beautiful." The word suddenly took a new meaning – a more pleasant one. It made me blush. It made me excited. I was crazy!

33

His name was Derrick.

One day, Derrick asked me if I could walk down to the next stop sign later in the day when everyone in my house was sleep and I did just that! I couldn't wait to talk to him as soon as the brightness in the sky cleared away. We smoked weed all through the first hour and rode around in his car.

Something about the taste of the weed he gave me was different from the one my uncle had let me smoke. It had a funny taste to it. Something felt odd, but I was not an expert; I pretended as if nothing was wrong. But deep down, the weed made me feel funny and weird in a way I never felt before. I was in this state until we ended up at a hotel after riding down various streets. When I woke up, I was naked. There was blood on the sheets and he was beside me, naked too.

Derrick told me that I became a woman that night. I wished I had enough time to worry about his words, but it was a new day and I hadn't slept at home. I missed school and I knew my grandmother would be worried sick about me. I shamefully clutched the sheets of the bed to my naked chest and I asked the first man who took my virginity to take me home to my grandmother.

"No."

It was the simple word Derrick had said to my request. He further told me that he wouldn't be able to take me home because I was too young to be with him in the first place.

"A lot of people would know that I was with you throughout the night, beautiful," he whispered, gritting his teeth in concern, more for him than for me.

The thing was that I knew absolutely nothing about him, but I liked the words he had initially told me. I pondered about it briefly as he spoke, and I realized that I had wanted to be a woman for a long time. I suddenly wanted to know how it felt to be one… again.

I was only diving deep into more regretful things and I didn't know. My curiosity probably was the problem, or perhaps the fact that I was a bit selfish. I thought of myself alone. I had thought of my grandmother briefly and since he told me he couldn't take me there, she was no longer a problem. I delved right back to his words that pleased me. More than being selfish, I was a pleasure-seeking child who redefined herself as an adult the moment she was with a man.

Derrick and I had sex that morning before I left and everything about it felt euphoric. It was a feeling I had never felt before and I liked it! I was tired of living in a house full of boys and not having a fun of my own. Sex was it; it was the fun I had been missing out from.

As I walked home from the hotel that morning, I couldn't stop smiling. In my head, I thought of

36

Derrick as my boyfriend – the secret type of boyfriend that I had done things with which no one else in school or girls my age had ever done.

When I got home, my grandmother was already so worried about me. She had filed a police report to declare me missing and had thought that something terrible had happened to me. When she saw me, she yelled at me and demanded to know where I had gone, tears running down her cheeks and for the first time, I felt that I needed to be far away from her. I needed to run. I needed to leave home.

It was the first time that I thought of running away. When I left with Derrick, I didn't know I was going to consider not ever going back nor did I know I would be out all night. *I am a woman now and there is nothing anybody could say different to me*, I told myself. *I can take care of myself now.*

I couldn't leave the house anyway. I didn't have Derrick's number or even know if I would see him

37

again. I let my grandmother scream at the top of her voice for long without muttering a word. I left for my room afterwards. I marked this episode finished in my mind.

A few days later, Derrick showed up to get his car fixed again. This time, he said he needed an oil change. Of course, he didn't say this to me but immediately I had noticed him around, I rushed to where he met with Uncle Freddie and listened to every conversation. I also pretended to be watching my uncle fix the car. Derrick told my uncle his number had changed and as he gave my Uncle his new number, aloud, my ears picked on every number. Even as I did this, I was afraid I was going to lose the number anytime soon. Fortunately for me, my uncle asked me to grab a pen and paper from inside the house and write the number down for him and I asked myself, *does Derrick want me to have the number too?* I believed he did. I wrote the number down in a separate paper, making a mental note to call him later in the day.

I called him later that night and he sounded as if he was happy to hear from me. Loud music was playing in the background and I assumed that he was riding in his car since it was similar to what happened the night we were together.

Derrick asked me to meet him again that night and I acceded to do so without blinking. I knew that it would hurt my grandmother. After the night I hadn't come home, she got me to promise her the morning I returned that I would never scare her like that again. But when it came to Derrick now, I seldom thought about other people's feelings – my grandmother's inclusive. I liked the thought of being with him again, so I chose to meet him.

I slid quietly out of the house when everyone was asleep, and Derrick took me to the same hotel. I told him I didn't want to smoke though. I just wanted to be in his presence and enjoy his company. It wasn't as if I liked how the marijuana made me feel. I let him pour me a cup of alcohol instead.

Accompanying words with action seems to be one of the hardest things to do for people, especially for youngsters. As adamant as I was that I wouldn't smoke and as willing as Derrick was to oblige me, I ended up asking him to pass me one of his rolls of marijuana. I couldn't resist the smoke that slithered out of his lips nor could I resist the enthralling smell of marijuana that took over the room.

So, I eventually smoked in a nutshell and it had the same taste as the last time we smoked together. This time, I stayed awake, my eyes trailing the length of his arms and the thinness of his lips.

I was turned on just by the sight of him. We had sex again and he touched and kissed places on my body that he missed the first time. While his hands were on my skin, he told me so many things he liked about me. He used endearing words. He made me feel special and by the time he made love to me, I felt an irredeemable lust for him.

That night, at the age of twelve, I realized two things about the first man that slept with me. One, he was eighteen-years older. Two, he was married with children.

My feelings were hurt!

I couldn't bear to look Derrick in the face. I grunted for as long as I could while he lifted himself off me and smoked some more.

He drove me to a nearby store when we were done, and I walked the rest of the way.

When I got home, my grandmother was angrier than the first time. She instantly knew I wasn't the same anymore. She knew I wasn't the kid she

41

used to know. The next morning, she took me to a doctor and found out that I was sexually active. I was immediately placed on birth control and I could remember lying about who I was sleeping with.

I told my grandmother that I had been sleeping with a boy in my class from school. I couldn't tell her it was a grown man and that he came to our home frequently. I wouldn't dare! Especially since I could see it in her eyes that I was hurting her. The doctors also told her that there was cocaine and marijuana in my system as well. I knew I hadn't touched any cocaine but oh, I surely had an idea on how it got in my system.

After the appointment with the doctor, my grandma didn't want me to go outside anymore. She got everyone in the neighborhood to watch every move I made. Derrick desperately began to call the house since he didn't have access to me anymore but often hung up whenever someone else picked his call. He wanted me to pick up but unfortunately, I wasn't even allowed to go near any object of communication in the house. I wanted to get to him just as badly as he wanted to get to me.

But he had a wife! I reminded myself.

At some point, I promised myself that I wouldn't talk to him anymore. I would find a boy my age and we would grow up together and get married, I thought. Well, the truth was that boys my age that I knew were not having sex yet. More so, the slightly older boys who were teenagers knew my uncles and brothers and were afraid to talk to me. So, it was a matter of time before I figured out my decision to find a boy my age was only a fantasy, yet to be forgotten.

Finally, one day, while walking home from school, Derrick drove by me. I knew it was him because he pulled over to the gas station I told him I go to everyday to get candy after school. By this time, one of my brothers was walking with me from school. I couldn't say anything to Derrick and he sure couldn't say anything to me either. He brought our candy and sodas and I was trying to pretend as if I was still mad with him about his marriage.

Who was I fooling? No one.

Derrick was a man who knew I was a little girl he had introduced to womanhood and it would be hard not to want more of him. I ended up going home that night and all I could think about was him – how enticing he smelled and how he made me feel so adored the last time we were together.

I called him back that night and a woman picked up the phone. My heart was torn. I had given myself to him and he was married with his own family. My thirteenth birthday was approaching, and I wanted to spend it with him. I wanted him to be the man who would make the day so memorable.

I was so angry that he wasn't the one that picked my call that I stole my grandmother's car and tried to drive to the hotel that we had made love twice. Of course, I didn't know how to drive, so I wrecked the car instead and almost lost my life. I remember the police putting me in handcuffs and saying my grandmother had reported the car stolen and her granddaughter as a runaway.

I had thought the worst that could happen was to go home and my grandmother would be upset as she normally would. That didn't happen! Not this time!

I was going to jail for being an incorrigible child and for stealing a car.

What had gotten into me? Where had I gone wrong? I sincerely didn't have answers then, but I felt betrayed and hurt at the same time. I found out that I craved alcohol terribly. I wanted weed at all cost, but they didn't have this in jail.

While in there, I couldn't make phone calls the first night. It was weekend and court was not accessible until Monday. This was to decide if the judge was sending me home or not. All I could think about was Derrick. *Is he missing me as I was missing him? Would the cops let me go home or I would I be here for a while?* My mind was filled with thoughts about my grandmother's feelings or about myself but about Derrick. I was comfortably heading down a road of destruction.

The weekend passed slowly and finally, it was time for me to appear in court. My grandmother was there, and she broke down into tears as she saw me in shackles and cuffs. She was asked to testify about my behavior and about the truth of her stolen car and she spoke softly, tears dripping down her cheeks. It was as if there was so much pain in her voice. She was hurt that I had caused her so much embarrassment. I didn't care. I was mad at her too!

I focused on the anger that I felt for her because she reported the car that I had taken as stolen. How could she do that to the granddaughter she claimed to love? It was even more shocking when the judge asked her to speak and all she could do was to ask them to keep me.

She told them it was better for me that way!

I listened angrily as my grandmother told the judge that she hardly knew where I was at night and often lost sleep, thinking I could have been murdered by a lowlife scoundrel. Listening to her and not considering that I had anything to input, the judge sentenced me to forty-five days in prison. The thirteenth birthday I looked forward to spending with my lover, I now had to spend it in jail – for forty-five days! This was the first reality that hit me. I was so angry with my grandmother that I immediately felt pure hatred for her.

After everything, I was transferred to a juvenile detention center. I wasted my life there, despite how short my term was. I got into two fights and learned nothing despite that I was forced to go to school in there. The night before I was to return to court, I threw urine in a girl's face and got sent to lock up. I felt miserable every second. I had nowhere to run to anymore. I didn't have the fun I was used to anymore. I wasn't able to sneak out of a house anymore to meet someone at a stop sign nor could I talk to who I wanted to talk to.

My grandmother was the only visitor I had and every time that she visited, I could see sadness in her eyes. She saw how the place made me bitter and angry. When it was time to go back before the judge, she presented herself before the judge and asked that I should be brought back home. I had made her several false promises to do right and not engage in the same activities anymore and I think these encouraged her to plead my case.

Her plea fell on deaf ears though. Unknown to us, staff of the detention center evaluated me throughout the entire time I was in and reported back to the court. They recommended that I wasn't fit to be out yet and needed to stay an additional forty-five days without getting into fights or disrespecting anyone. What? How could anyone survive that? I felt my world torn before my very eyes.

At the end of the hearing, the judge sentenced me to another six months and I was headed back to the horrible place that I thought I would escape forever.

CHAPTER THREE

My New Life in Juvenile Detention Center

Life, one should know, isn't always one-directional. One moment, you are free and happy and the next moment, you are in chains – perhaps limited by a phase in life that you haven't anticipated.

Out of this context – or perhaps still in tandem with it – the cheerful life you are used to could also surprise you by suddenly becoming unpleasant. You find out that people that you have gotten used to are no longer available. The love that you feel from them and for yourself disappear and you feel alone. You feel as if everything doesn't work for you anymore. And at the end, you fall into a deep depression – a constant reminder that you have terribly failed.

The realization of this new phase in your life is one of the crucial moments of development. It takes you down a narrow path where your thoughts would be here and there – between the calculations of giving up or trying once again. You might have been in this position before, or perhaps you haven't.

But I know I had and the first feeling I felt was extreme hatred for everyone, especially my grandmother. I was being taken back to jail and this time around, as it dawned on me that I wouldn't be there for a short while but for six whole months, I began to feel deep sated hatred for her. I expected that she could have done more – cry perhaps or tell the judge how I had always been a good kid before I suddenly felt the need to be independent – but she didn't do all these.

She just sat there and let them take me away, I thought bitterly to myself, swearing. *She is so evil. She doesn't care a rat's behind that I could have*

51

died in the car or that jail could be far worse for someone my age. The judge is also wrong to have treated me this way. I had only stolen a car and had even almost died in it.

Apart from the growing anger inside of me, the truth was that I wasn't ready to leave the life I was used to behind and go to jail. I knew what it meant for me. There would be no more freedom to do what I wanted. It definitely also meant that I couldn't smoke anymore. No one was allowed to drink either in jail and I was furious that everything that could make me deal with what I was going through was going to be taken away from me.

The realization of these fueled my anger and fury. I was furious at life. I stared at the strange faces of everyone in jail and all I could feel was bitterness, bias and resentment as if each of them had contributed to what I was going through.

In the first few days that I spent in jail before I was shipped to the main juvenile facility, Grandma visited but I refused to see her. I knew how I could lose myself in my own anger and rant aggressively at her. And while I wished I could do it and get it over with, I also knew it was unwise to do so after being sent to jail for the same aggressive behavior.

So, I forgot about my grandmother in a nutshell. When I was picked up and taken to the main juvenile facility, I swore to myself that I would forever hate her. I also thought briefly about my brothers and wondered if they would be doing fine at home without me. I was their sister. We were supposed to spend our lives together, and now this wasn't going to happen anymore. I was being separated from the only people that I loved dearly, and it felt like hell just thinking about how much I will miss them already.

I called home after I was shipped to the facility and the first news I got was that Jody had also been sent to the boys' juvenile jail for stealing cars. I felt sick inside instantly. More anger steamed inside of me and this time around, it was for my own selfishness. I felt that I had been so concerned with pleasuring myself all the time that I was free that I hadn't focused on my younger brothers. While I had gone wild, they were probably doing the same until we were finally forced to face the consequences of our actions.

Like me, Jody would have to be thrown into a strange world, one he wouldn't be able to easily adapt to. I thought about this and it made me numb. I thought about our little brother too and how he would be so lonely at home with grandmother and her husband and once again, I felt angry at myself. I hadn't looked out for everyone as I should have as their sister. I was irresponsible – there was no other word to describe me and I was willing to accept this fault of mine with teary eyes. I loved my brothers and it seemed I had terribly failed them.

In the juvenile facility, we were treated like army recruits. We had to wake up very early in the morning and make our beds. Daily head count was done to make sure everyone was in bed and often, officials were rude to us. They spoke to us and treated us as if we didn't have families of our own. It was if we were going to spend the rest of our lives in the facility if we didn't act according to their wishes.

As if the rude officials weren't enough to get me riled up, the inmates were constant trouble too. They fought all the time on the slightest provocation. They fought about food, about their cells, about words that were said to each other – basically, everyone was looking for a way to lash out at the other girl with all the anger each had within themselves.

55

This new life suddenly got me falling into deep depression. I wasn't often unhappy. I had no such experiences of aggression before. Sometimes, I confined myself to my cell and thought about the freedom that I had enjoyed before. I was forced to go to school now and while I hated to go, I didn't have a choice than to do so. Soon, I began to consider my past and all the things I could have done differently which could have made the present a bit different.

The food in the juvenile jail was one of the reasons I hated the place. It was horrible. Sometimes, I was given a bowl for my breakfast and I would stare at it for long and feel a tear gliding down my cheeks. I deserved a better life, I told myself. No matter what I had done, this life wasn't what I should have gotten. In an attempt to make myself better, I often gave out my food to the other inmates. I felt that I could starve myself to death – this was better since no one loved me anymore.

I missed my brothers the entire time I was in there. I missed waking them up and getting them ready for school. I missed seeing them around the house and laughing with them too and all the while that I thought about them, I didn't think about my grandmother once. It was as if she had slipped off my mind permanently. I understand now that she wanted the best for me, or perhaps I understood this then too, but I still blamed her for my situation nonetheless. I felt that she didn't consider other options to punish me for my mistakes.

I met a lot of girls in the facility but the one I quickly bonded with was my roommate, Dominic. She was about the same age as me; she didn't have many friends, even in jail. She told me that she hadn't had sex with men before but confessed that she had smoked a lot of weed and marijuana and that she drank a lot. Our conversations were mostly about sex and it is surprising how we talked about it till late in the night.

It was during one of our conversations that Dominic told me that she was homosexual. It meant that she felt attracted to only women and had had sex with them only. She had an inmate girlfriend in the facility, too, and she told me that they often fondled each other when no one was looking. Being in jail had introduced her to homosexuality and she wasn't ashamed of it.

One night, after the routine checkup by the jail officials, Dominic came down from her bed to meet me at the lower bunk and we kissed and fondled each other. It was my first kiss – since Derrick had never done that before when we had sex – and I have to admit, I felt pleasured by it coming from a girl. That night changed my sexual orientation. Dominic and I didn't know what we were doing but I felt that I liked men and women now. I felt that I was attracted to both gender and it wasn't a terrible thing.

I was in the dorm weeks after this incident when I was suddenly called to go to the infirmary. This was the popular medication unit in the facility and I was a bit confused that I was required to go there. I wasn't ill neither had I sustained an injury. I was scheduled to meet a psychiatrist instead who initially wanted to know why I was giving my food away. Apparently, the jail had thought I was trying to hurt myself by starving to death and equally hurt others by giving out food that I thought could harm them.

I was confounded at first. It was at that period that I realized that I had the power to do both – hurt myself and hurt others. To be frank, I didn't really feel good thinking about it. It only felt quite exhilarating to know that I could be considered a threat to the other girls in the jail.

59

The psychiatrist that I met wanted me to have weekly sessions with her. According to her, our sessions would make me feel better and it could also convince the judge on my next hearing that I was trying my best to behave. I didn't have a choice anyway, so I began to have sessions with her twice in a week.

The first session I had with her lasted for more than an hour and I could remember that our discussion was more about my mum and family. During each session, she made notes and asked various personal questions that made me realize that she knew more than I knew about my own family. She spoke in detail - stories probably recounted to her by my grandmother. For instance, it was through her questions that I was reminded that my mother's boyfriend was the one that murdered her. Of course, I had known this as a child but the reality of it never really struck me hard as it did when she spoke about it. It was obvious that she wanted to know if this incident affected my thoughts and behavior as I grew up, and if I blamed myself for not being old enough to do anything.

I was able to pour out my anger and frustrations during these sessions. I spoke about how I hated everyone because they had bonds with a mother or father that I never had. I also expressed how I had often thought about how mother had died without having anyone to help her. I questioned how she couldn't scream at the top of her lungs for help or even cry out to God to help her.

I was at a breaking point there. I had begun to accept some of the incidents in my life and also making meanings from them. I don't know what the psychiatrist's goal was, but I knew that taking me down memory lane got me in touch with my emotional being. It made me understand how much I had known but had been unwilling to accept. Perhaps if a lot of people could get in

61

touch with their emotional being, they would understand the reasons for the path that they had chosen for themselves over time.

I was given a medication for depression the next morning after my first session, which helped to calm my emotions. I began to smile often. I wasn't angry anymore and I was surprised at how a pill could effectively control my anger. Since male and female inmates shared the same infirmary, I also saw my brother while I was being administered the medication. Seeing him made me cry. He didn't look happy and seemed so lost amongst boys who were a bit older than he was.

I felt irresponsible again for not being able to take care of him. I felt like a failure. I had failed my mother, my brothers, my grandmother and everyone who had thought that I was going to turn out fine. I was unable to talk to Jody and I didn't know if that felt worse than the guilt that I felt, considering that I had been unable to look out for him.

The medication I was given was my only escape from this deep sadness. Since it often helped to make me calm, I realized that I could be different. I began to channel my energy into something else - positivity. I suddenly felt the need to be better...to be happier. I felt that I needed to use them as I was told to so that I could stop getting angry at everyone, or at myself.

Coincidentally, Grandma came to visit me at the same time. It was six weeks after I had begun to use the drugs and I felt quite elated that she had come. I hadn't seen her in months either. So, I hugged her compassionately, sat in front of her and watch her cry as she expressed how sad she was every day that Jody and I wasn't home where we belonged.

She brought me some chicken from one of my favorite places and I cried, too, remembering how

63

much she tried to take care of everyone, despite the difficulty she faced at her age. I promised her that I would be better now. I told her about the medication and how I was finally getting better. I also promised to never see boys anymore once I was back home. Right there, we both resolved that I would do everything to make sure that I never smoke or drink again. Grandma cried all through and finally left after hugging me again. She had come to see Jody too and I couldn't help but imagine the effort she had put into seeing us, despite her work shifts.

Once the new week started, I began to go to school with renewed determination. While I hadn't concentrated on getting good grades before, my perspective had changed now. I was no longer angry. If I still was, I told myself that I would channel it into becoming a better person. Doing so was one of the best ways to achieve greatness and it is quite surprising that I learned this at a young age.

My grades became better afterwards. I had an A in every subject, higher than all the females who were now shocked that I could do so well. I asked questions in class and I often finished my assignments on time. I would sit at the dorm with these assignments, feeling eager to study the topics and to take my findings to class the next day. My grandmother's visit had simply made a positive impact on me and I wasn't ready to let go of it.

At some point, I realized that if I could be better in juvenile jail, I could do better outside. So, I participated in all psychiatrist treatment and did better with the girls. Quickly, I made new friends and became happy with my life once more.

Six months finally passed, and I was back to where I had started – in chains and in route to see the judge again. I could remember this day vividly because it was the first time that I prayed. The jail official had escorted me to the floor beneath the courthouse and I had bowed my head in prayer. I prayed to God for forgiveness. I told him that I wouldn't do the terrible things that I had done in the past. I wanted to change, and I asked for his guidance.

When the court officer finally came to take me to the courtroom, I was terribly nervous. I walked beside him, holding my breath and letting memories of the past few months flash through my mind. I didn't want to go back. I wanted to go back home to my family…to be free and happy one again.

Grandma was in the courthouse, too, and a smile was on her face as if she knew I was finally coming home to her. I suddenly had the same feeling too. I heaved a long sigh, shuddered happily and waited for the judge to speak. While he did, I also remembered that before I left the facility, I had been directed to pack my stuff. It felt as if everyone was trying to tell me it was time for me to go home and I had been too nervous to see it. Everything was finally going to be fine. I was having my life back.

The judge released me on probation. He ordered that I was to take random drug test and must always be at home at a certain time. I was to also remain on medication and should have scheduled sessions with a psychiatrist at home. If grandma reported me to the court again, I would be back in juvenile and there would be no escape for me for a very long time.

None of these conditions bothered me. I was only excited to be granted back my freedom. It meant that I could see my family again. My brothers too! I nodded mutely as the conditions were read out to me and in another hour, I was heading back home.

Grandma was the one that drove me back home. The entire time, it was obvious that she was excited, too. She told me how she missed having me at home and also wanted to know if we were on the same page. She asked if I knew what I would do once I got back and also began to mention all the chores I could get busy with.

As I listened to her and as we got nearer to our home, I felt a bit of anxiety taking over my thoughts. I thought about all the things I had promised not to do, and I realized that I might just get back to them. I suddenly felt the desire to do so.

I missed Derrick, too, and the first instinct I had immediately the car inched towards the front porch of our home was to call him.

Perhaps going through juvenile jail had been for nothing.

CHAPTER FOUR

Drugs, Lies, Sex and Crime

It was obvious that Grandma was happy that I had been finally released from juvenile detention center. When we got home, she had dinner set for me and everything in the house looked as if she had stayed up all night to make sure they were clean.

In exchange for her gesture, I stayed out of trouble the first week, got home in time and even made a new friend – Sasha. Sasha was two years older than me and always had boys over without her mom bickering about it. We clicked instantly and began to hang out together.

While everything could have gone on normal from there, I met Jeremiah, and everything changed. He was Sasha's cousin and I would go to her house just to meet him, so we could be alone. He was in a gang and to me then, this was so sexy and validating for a man. Jeremiah had a lot of respect in the streets and being his *chick (at least I thought I was)* would probably earn me a lot of respect as well. Within the first few days that I got to know him, Jeremiah got me a fake ID card that could grant me access to clubs and for the first time, I knew how it felt to be in a club with lots of men and women who drank, used hard drugs and smoked without limit.

The first night that I went to the club with him was amazing. The loud music, the strippers, the drinks; everything made me feel like a superstar. Everyone, including Sasha and my home girl, Lisa, that went with us, took Ecstasy pills. Jeremiah was with his gang members half of the night and at some point, he came to me and told me to come outside with him to the car.

When I did, he closed the doors shut and handed me a bag of cocaine. Although, I had never used cocaine before, I placed the straw up my nostril and snorted it, loving the funny feeling that slid down my throat. It wasn't as bad as I thought it would be but certainly, the high it gave made me feel good.

Afterwards, Jeremiah handed me a small gun and told me to lay it in the seat of my underwear and enter the club with it. Unlike the men, women were just being patted down into the club without being thoroughly searched. And when I was able to successfully get into the club with the gun, Jeremiah happily fed me cocaine all night. I also popped Ecstasy pills and drank countless shots of Hennessy – all of which I never knew would have so much control over me.

I was around fourteen years old by this time, but my fake ID card said I was twenty-two years old. It meant I could take as many shots of hard drugs as any adult would. This night was also the first one I didn't make it home on time in accordance with the judge's instructions. I figured: "I'm already going to be in trouble, so why not make the best of it?"

We didn't leave the club until around 7am and it was a night I vowed never to forget. Jeremiah never used the gun that night and now, I believe he just needed it for protection in case something was to happen. The experience of that night, however, broke me to a point where things went farther downhill.

This has always been the case in our lives. There is that point – a breaking point – where things worsens or suddenly becomes better. For the former, most of us do not know these breaking points while a lot of us do. For me, thinking about everything now, I think I had a lot of breaking points. I was just too focused on pleasing myself that I didn't notice them.

I didn't go back home; neither did I go to Sasha's house after I left the club. I knew my grandmother had probably been looking for me and had notified the court that I was in violation of my release. I also had lots of drugs in my system and there was no way I would pass a drug test. So, Jeremiah and I went to a hotel where we continually used more hard drugs and where we stayed for weeks, since I was too afraid to go back home and be sent back to juvenile jail.

Clubbing became my life weekly and sometimes daily. I also did whatever Jeremiah wanted so I could stay with him. At some point though, he was gone for days and I became worried. I called him several times to see where he was and didn't get an answer or response. I panicked. I had no money, no food and couldn't go home because I had officially run away, and no family knew where I was.

Desperate, I went to the club and began to dance with another guy, Craig, so I could have a place to sleep the night. I figured if he liked what he

73

saw, and I teased him enough, he would want to get a hotel, have sex and I would kill time until I found Jeremiah.

Well, it worked because I left with him for a hotel that night. We had sex, got high and had more sex. I didn't know anything about him and he had experienced the deeper parts of my body that were supposed to be for my husband. I felt so filthy and for a minute I was willing to go home and face the raft from my grandmother but when I thought about how deep I was in, I changed my mind fast.

Jeremiah never called back. I would call Sasha and she seemed like she was completely baffled that Jeremiah and I were even dealing with each other. I thought for a moment that they all were playing games with me because they knew my situation. How could she be upset with me or view me any differently since she was having sex at such age too?

74

When I woke up the next morning, Craig was gone, and I was due out of the hotel by 11 am. I couldn't go outside because someone may see me and call my uncles. People in the streets were already telling me that my uncles had come by, threatening people and looking for me but Jeremiah had people lying that I wasn't nowhere around town and that nobody had seen me.

Now, I needed to get money somehow so that I could survive since I had no intention of going home. I also wanted cocaine and didn't know how to get it. So, I washed all the filth from the night off of me and began to walk downtown Columbia. I was so lost, and I had nowhere to go but I knew one thing I had learned since being out in the world was that I was a female and men loved sex.

Luckily, they automatically thought that I was a prostitute as I walked, so they honked their horns while some would pull over and ask if I needed a ride. I hadn't eaten all day and I needed food as well. During the day, I stopped at several waffle houses and gas stations to rest or to get bottled water. At one of the houses, I was approached by another guy with dreads. He offered to ride around, and smoke weed with me all night and I agreed, finally seeing that I didn't have a choice anymore.

We smoked, laughed and of course, like every other man I met before him, he wanted sex as well. He also wanted it in his car as if I was a cheap prostitute, but I didn't let him. I ended up smoking his weed, drinking and reaching out to my home girl, Lashae. Lashae and I always called each other cousins while we grew up. We were more like sisters since I told her my darkest secrets and she never repeated them to anyone. When I called her, I explained to her what I had been through and she offered to sneak me into the house that night, so I could rest. I would however need to be out or up hiding by the time her mom got up for work.

Lashae wasn't into all the street stuff but that night, I reeled her into my mess. I hadn't spent a minute in the house when Jeremiah surprisingly called me. He wanted us to meet but I argued against this, intending to make him understand that what he did was wrong. Lashae, however, convinced me to and even offered me something out of her closet to wear. She got dressed, too, and we met Jeremiah at the stop sign.

Because Jeremiah knew that I had Lashae with me, he decided to bring one of his homeboys with him that night too. She had never stayed out of her mom's house, so here I was being a bad example to a good friend and causing someone else's mother pain just to have a friend with me.

Lashae didn't have an ID card to get into the club so we couldn't go there. We went to a hotel room and I had sex with Jeremiah and she had sex at

77

the same time with his friend on a bed beside mine. She however went home afterwards, her mom probably not noticing that she was gone, but I couldn't go anywhere. My only option was to make Jeremiah happy, so he could make sure I had a place to sleep each night.

Though Jeremiah paid the hotel bill for the night, I wasn't sure I would deal with him anymore. He was acting unreliable and at that point, I was ready to go home or find another way to fend for myself. At this time, Myspace was active, so I created a fake Myspace page and started reaching out to men there. I knew in order to get money, I would have to offer myself to them. The next two weeks, I slept with over ten different men and made money to keep my hotel room.

This became a very dangerous and ruinous part of my life. I overused drugs. I had become a full-time prostitute and I became depressed, too. I missed my brothers and I had stopped the depression medicine all together. My life was a disaster and I knew it. I was tired, and my body was worn, and I needed rest.

So, I finally called my grandmother.

*****

Grandma broke down on the other end of the phone as soon as she heard my voice. I remember hearing my uncles screaming in the background, grateful that I wasn't dead. She promised she would go with me to turn myself in for probation and that I should come home. She wasn't mad anymore; she was happy to know that I wasn't hurt and that I was safe.

I went home and when I got there, the police pulled up a few minutes later. I was headed back to juvenile detention center and I knew it. I wasn't sure how long I would be there this time, but I knew it was over for me.

I went before a different judge the next day. I didn't have any words for anyone. I couldn't apologize because I wouldn't mean it if I did. I just wanted to have fun and it got way out of hand – this had always been the truth.

The judge sentenced me to an indeterminate sentence. That meant that I could remain in their custody until my twenty-first birthday, depending on how well or bad I did. I wasn't going to a jail-like facility; I was going to a group home and it was almost two miles from the last facility that I was at. Because of this phase of my life, I never made it to see my brother, Jody, during his incarceration. My brother, Frank, barely knew me because I was never home to even create a bond with him. I was back in the hands of the State of South Carolina and I really didn't care.

I adjusted well at the group home though. We could wear regular clothes and we went to school on campus like the detention center. It really felt more like a foster home than a jail. While there, I got really close to a worker who was named Mrs. Litty. She was the fun one who tried to allow us to make the best of our situation. She would dance with us and we would sing and have fun. I felt like a child again without the drugs. Mrs. Litty took me in and we bonded like a mother and daughter. I would open up to her about my life and she would share her stories with me as well. I felt like she had a passion for helping children and it wasn't all work to her.

Another woman that I bonded with – my God mother, Amy – was a supervisor for the Juvenile jail and she had gotten word that I was back in jail. She came to visit me once and basically let me know that I had disappointed her. Apparently, there was so many people counting on me and I wasn't even counting on myself. If only many people in the world knew this, perhaps they would do better than they already did in life.

I did what I had to do to get out of the group home. One month turned into two and two turned into three and briskly, I was sixteen years old before I came home. So much had changed by the time I did. Jody and Frank were taller and older, and they greeted me in tears as soon as they saw me. Their big sister was finally home again. Of course, everybody felt like it was only a matter of time before I screwed up again.

Perhaps I also had the same thought. We all had that point that we doubted ourselves.

I, however, tried everything I could not to go against probation or violate the conditions of my release. I was assigned a female probation officer and she was so rude. I felt like she was waiting patiently for me to mess up, so she could send me back. She popped up at my house randomly and tested me for drugs. She called my grandmother like clockwork to check in on me. All this time, I was a teenager who had experienced what most adults had not, but I was determined to do better in life.

Or so I thought….

*****

My uncle was still fixing cars in the yard of the house. Years have passed, and he was now fixing cars full time. More so, men still visited his shed and one of them, Melvin, often stared intently at me. Melvin was clean cut, older and spoke with such good tone and charisma. I could tell he was interested in me and wanted to talk so I spoke first.

My uncle told me he had just been recently released from prison. To me, that was good news because it only meant he had no woman or the woman he had left while he was back there was no longer around – so he was looking to start over.

After the previous experiences with men I had, I wasn't too happy to talk to another man that was getting their car fixed. For some strange reason though, this felt different. Melvin and I exchanged numbers and I conversed with him over the phone for a few weeks prior to meeting up with him. I could tell he was into the street life as well because he didn't have a job but always had money.

I was sixteen now and my grandmother wasn't hard on me as she was before. I had a little bit of freedom too. Melvin and I met up a few weeks later and drove around the city. We stopped at a Waffle house a few times to eat and soon, this became our regular routine. At the time, I found out his mother was sick with cancer; we spent several of our days together at his aunt's house, visiting her.

I didn't tell Melvin my real age. I told him I was eighteen and he believed me. He didn't propose to have sex with me either. For my seventeenth birthday (which he thought was my nineteenth birthday), he took me out and we had sex for the first time. He taught me how to drive, brought my clothes for school and we bonded really fast. I felt like I was falling in love for the first time. I hadn't experienced that before and it felt good to have one person to confide in as well as to spend time with daily.

Because of wanting to be close to Melvin, I dropped out of school and never went back. All I wanted to do was spend time with him and I couldn't do that while I went to school. He was upset I didn't finish school, but we had been making goals to be a family already. He told me he had no kids and I believed him.

When I turned seventeen, I moved out of my grandmother's house. By this time, my youngest brother, Frank, had caught a burglary charge and was sent to prison. My other brother, Jody, was back in jail as well with different drug charges. My uncles were living their lives as well and time was just passing us all by.

I moved with Melvin into his mom's old house. We did everything together. He taught me the proper way to drive, took me to get my driver's license and purchased my first car for me. Everything felt good at the moment. My life seemed to be getting better than it started out. I was introduced to his family and everyone seemed to be good, especially his aunt Jessie. I also finally told him my real age. We took trips all over the US and visited his sister in Virginia frequently. Even my grandmother and uncles welcomed him with open arms. I had a man of my own and I was finally happy. I felt like this was a story that was never going to end.

When I turned eighteen years old, I was head over hills in love with Melvin. He could ask me to jump off a bridge and I probably would have at his command. Then, one night, as we were laying in bed, I smelled myself and it didn't smell right. Any woman knows her body scent and this scent on me was a fishy smell. I immediately called him and told him I needed to go to a doctor. Besides the smell, I had been feeling nauseated as well. When we got to the hospital, the doctors tested me and told me that I was pregnant. Not only was I pregnant but I had contracted an STD.

I hadn't been with anyone else since my release from prison. Melvin was the only man that could have given me any disease. I looked at him in the hospital and he looked baffled as to what was going on. I was glad that I was pregnant, but I was also sad to realize that he had been having unprotected sex. I was prescribed medicine to take to cure the STD and we left the hospital that night. I was lost for words instead of being happy. The man I loved so much and who I was now carrying a child for, was not faithful to me.

87

I remember going home and packing my things, threatening to go back to my grandmother's house. He begged me not to leave and admitted to cheating and even told me who he cheated with. To my surprise, it wasn't somebody I didn't know –it was a friend of mine who I had introduced him to. Not only did he admit to that, but he told me at this point that this wasn't his first child. He said he was also dealing with a married woman by the name of Angelica. She had just given birth to a little girl and he wasn't sure if her child was his or her husband's.

It was a lot of information to take in at the time. This time was one of the saddest moments in my life. Melvin went to the clinic and got treated for the STD while I spent a week at my grandmother's house. However, after many flowers, candy, apologies and gifts I went back home with him. He seemed to be excited about the baby on the way and so was I.

Angelica, the woman that was pregnant for him, called often in the night and wanted him to see the child. This caused a disagreement between us since Melvin seemed to have accepted the child as his. Also, during the first trimester of my pregnancy, I spent countless days and nights getting threatened through phone calls from private numbers. I was so angry with him. I felt like he was lying to Angelica and I or perhaps, there was more to him and her than he was telling me.

Why couldn't he just get a blood test and see if the child was his or not? Why keep dealing with a married woman who had already proven to be disloyal to her husband and allow her to cause confusion in our home? There were so many unanswered questions and every single one drove me down the path of sadness, anger and depression.

Angelica would also seldom come by the house unannounced, looking for him when he didn't answer the phone and I knew they were still dealing around. She hated me so much that she lied to his family that she left her baby with us and I burned her with a cigarette. I couldn't even smoke when I was in my first trimester because the taste made me sick.

Angelica was toxic to our relationship and I told Melvin that there had to be an ultimatum – either he got a blood test and figure out whether the child was his and we continue to be together or he would allow me to depart so he could continue to deal with this married woman who was a known whore in the community. In response, Melvin promised that he was done with her.

Getting farther along in my pregnancy, we found out we were having a girl. Melvin wanted me to name her after his mother, but Ethel was an older name. I decided to go with it anyway because those were his wishes. Melvin became an awesome father and he loved every breath Ethel took. He would spend nights, singing, kissing her and just looking into her big beautiful eyes. The first words he said to her when she entered the world was "You got those lips like your mama".

Thus, my little family seemed complete. I was happy to be a new mom and Angelica was no longer harassing me or causing confusion. She was out of the picture... or so I thought.

I got a job in a gas station after having my daughter and Melvin was still doing what he was doing on the streets. Things were different now that we had a child. We moved out of his mother's home into an apartment and a year later, I was already expecting another child.

I found out around this time that my grandmother had been diagnosed with cancer.

*****

91

When my grandmother broke the news that she was battling breast cancer, my heart was torn. Again, it dawned on me that I had failed her as a grandchild. Her health had been dwindling and she was always around, trying to make me a better human. She went to chemo treatments and had surgery after surgery. I was pregnant with a second child at the time and I had no idea Melvin was out there cheating again. I also fell so sick that I quit my job and stayed home in bed all day.

I began to get depressed again due to the circumstances around me. Melvin was now barely home to help with Ethel and I was going to doctors' appointments alone with the new pregnancy. Everything seemed to have changed. I didn't have the same excitement that I had when I was pregnant for the first time. I had no help except from my cousin who had helped with my first baby shower and Lashae, who now had a child of her own and her own relationship.

It was obvious that Melvin and I were going into a direction where we could no longer be in a relationship. So, I prepared my mind for a stage where I could take care of my children alone. Subsequently, I gave birth to another baby girl – this was on February 12, 2007. She was so beautiful and looked identical to Ethel. Because of the childbirth, I started to gain weight but hardly paid attention to it.

As time went on, we moved out of the apartment we stayed in; it was a government-assist apartment and the office got news that I had a man living with me, so I was asked to leave. We got a new place and paid full rent. I also thought that I needed money to make sure that if Melvin ever went to jail, my kids would be taken care of. So, I found a job at the hotel, working with his cousin's girlfriend.

I was a front desk agent and I loved the job. It was less stressful, and I got to meet plenty of people. Besides, I was a mother now and real bills are rolling in, so I need to be able to pay them and take care of my children.

The new home we moved in was a mobile home in a trailer park. The floor in the living room had a big stain as if someone was murdered there and the blood was left in the middle of the floor. I hated that place, but I needed a place to lay my head and my children's head, so we maintained it. As time went on, Melvin and I had grown so distant with one another because our sex life wasn't the same. Either I was too tired from working or I knew he was out with other women and I was too angry with him to sleep with him. I felt like we were roommates now under the same roof raising two beautiful children.

One day, Melvin asked me: "What all of a sudden changed between us that all we do is argue"? My response to him was that when we first met, it was all about me. He fed me dreams and goals

94

that changed along the way. I was young, and he was older, so he basically molded me into what he wanted at home for his personal pleasures, but I wasn't the same little girl anymore. I had grown and so had he but in different directions.

While he was incarcerated, he practiced Islam and wanted me to be a Muslim as well. He would say this was the only way our relationship would work. My grandmother didn't pray to the same God he prayed to and when I was raised, we believed Jesus was our source – not Allah. Even though I wasn't an active Christian too, I believed in Jesus. So, converting because of him didn't happen.

Because of our different faith and because Melvin was an irredeemable cheat, he and I became enemies living under one roof. We argued day and night in front of the children, so much they would cry at the sight of us in the same room. We seldom fought physically, too.

95

I was just so angry that he had gotten me pregnant twice and had seemed like the man that would make me happy forever, only for him to do the exact opposite. He was still seeing Angelica and one time, she had deliberately left her panties in his car, so I could find it and become furious.

Because of these events, I became so cold hearted. I treated him nonchalantly and often wondered why he wouldn't be fair to me since I worked and took more than half the responsibilities at home. He got angry often at me and hated it that I didn't care much about it. When he left home angrily and didn't come for hours, I wouldn't even bother to call him.

Months later, at a time that I had just filed my income taxes and had a couple thousands of dollars, Melvin did the unspeakable. He was suddenly gone with the car and because I had no ride to get anywhere, I called a taxi, checked my dresser and found out that all my money was gone. Not only was the cash gone but I looked for my bank card which had all the rest of the money on it and it was gone too. He simply left me in the house, took all my money – a sum close to seven thousand dollars – and was nowhere to be found. He wouldn't even pick up my calls.

After he did this, I remember calling my uncle and asking him for gas money to get to work the next day. It was embarrassing but I didn't have a choice. I hadn't needed to ask my family for anything since I left my grandmother's house but now? Now, I needed help to pay rent, to take care of my children and to get to work and back to my home. I fell into another deep depression and really didn't know what to do. Often, I called his sister who resided in Virginia and she pretended like she had not heard from him. I even reached out to some of the women I knew he was sleeping with and they denied hearing from him as well.

My life changed when Melvin left. I felt what he did was more of mental abuse than anything. He simply wanted me to see that I could do nothing in life without him. I, in desperation for answers, called psychic hotlines to find possible explanations to why he did what he did too. This time of my life was the first I actually felt like giving up on life. It wasn't so much him being gone that had gotten me to this point, it was more so the situation I was left in. My job let me go because of so many call outs and my bills were behind. My lights got turned off and I received an eviction notice to vacate the residence we were living I couldn't take care of the children alone, too.

One day, I decided to end the suffering. I bought pain pills that I could use to take my life. I gave my babies a bath and put them to bed with no intention on seeing them again. I remember calling my cousin's mom, Karena, who lived not too far from where I lived and telling her I was tired. From my voice, she knew something was wrong. I didn't give her much information though before I hung up the call.

Afterwards, I unlocked my front door so that anyone could come in to take my children safely after they found my dead body. I showered, came back to the room and got ready to end my life. However, when I grabbed the bottle of pills, it fell out of my hand and rolled under the bed. As I was picking up each individual pill, I noticed a shoe box under the bed and quickly opened the lid to find Melvin's gun.

I felt that the gun was a sign that blowing my brains out was the route I should take instead of swallowing the pills. It obviously would make my death faster and painless. At the time that I pondered this, Karena kept calling me but I ignored the phone. I placed the gun on the side of

99

my face, pulled the trigger and it jammed. Nothing came out!

At the same time, my oldest daughter started to cry. Worried about her, I put the gun back in the box and ran to comfort her. For some reasons, she wouldn't go back to sleep; it seemed as if she knew something wasn't right with me.

Unfortunately, before I could get her to keep quiet, Karena scampered into the house through my front door, yelling for me. I came out of the room and she hugged me so hard and long and refused to leave me in that house alone. She had reached out to other family members and my grandmother showed up a few minutes later. She took my children and called an ambulance to check me out. I remember going to the emergency room and telling them the suicidal thoughts that I was having. I didn't tell them about the gun because I was afraid I would go to jail about it.

I was transferred to and admitted at the psychiatric ward of the hospital. I was given a psychiatrist who got me back on psychiatric medication and after seven days, I was finally allowed to go home. Upon my release, I found out that my grandmother had paid my rent for me. I had no idea how she did it, but I was grateful. Karena also had my children with her now and had gotten the lights back on. The kids were crawling and walking around happily, and it felt as if the life I had given up on could have meaning again.

Family and friends – I realized we all need them to be reminded why life is so beautiful and worth all the effort.

Grandma, especially, sat me down and told me that I needed to be a fighter to survive. She told me to fight through situations and never give up. She reminded me that I had two beautiful children who were looking up to me for survival. Ironically,

101

while at the hospital, I was tested and confirmed to be pregnant again. That was the third child on the way and the father was somewhere, lavishly spending all my money. I just had to do it, I told myself. I needed to listen to my grandmother and find a way to survive. I needed to be better than resorting to suicide.

Two months after, Melvin finally called to check on his children. When I realized it was him on the phone, I became angry again. I remember telling him I was pregnant again and how he asked if he could come home. I wanted to say no so badly but in spite of what he did, a part of me missed his presence. I missed having the help with the girls. I needed rest and having him in the house would be a great way to get some. So, I dumbly told him to come back home.

A day later, he walked through the door and there was complete silence. He saw that I had lost a few pounds from the stress and the look on his face said, "Now do you see how badly you need me"? The smirk on his face also reflected his intention to break me to the point where I served him and nobody else.

Surprisingly, he told me he didn't have any money left from my tax money and that he was just as broke as I was. I got confused and angry at the same time. I couldn't understand how one man could run through seven thousand dollars with no children to provide for and no bills?

Pondering this, I realized whatever he and I had was not love. It was going on five years with him and all we had accomplished were babies. Now, without money, we ended up moving out of the apartment into another apartment not too far away from my grandmother. My family, hearing that I had taken him back, was so upset with me.

Perhaps it didn't dawn on me soon enough. Melvin had taken everything I had and had returned with nothing. And I was proudly walking

103

around with a new pregnancy, as if the father and
I were on good terms.

CHAPTER FIVE

I Thought I Found What Was Missing…

At times, when life has dealt with you and showed you all its ugly side, you end up succumbing, knowing full well that no matter how much you fight, you are not getting out of its tight clutch easily.

I was already at that stage when I learnt of my new pregnancy. I was broke as anyone could be and jobless. To top it up was the fact that my kids dad didn't seem to care about how I got on with the pregnancy or even life in particular.

When I finally gave birth to my third child- a baby girl- on February 12, 2008 - the same day as the birthday of my second daughter, I felt at ease with life. A relieving feeling of completeness washed

105

over me and I felt the warmth of contentment rush through me. All self-pity that came with loneliness, emptiness, doubt and fear seemed to be replaced with inner peace. I had never felt as complete as I felt then. It was largely because of my three kids who I regarded as blessings to me.

With my kids with me, I felt like the strongest woman in the world. Even if I was not willing to be strong, I knew I just had to. My babies were looking up to me and I couldn't afford to let them down by showing signs of weakness. I had to be their Super-Woman.

Although my relationship with Melvin had dwindled to the point where it seemed as if sex was the only thing we still shared together, I still loved him anyway. I know it sounds crazy and perhaps stupid but every time I took a glance at my adorable kids, I couldn't help but remember that I was able to bring those angels into world because of Melvin. If he had helped in bringing my beautiful daughters into the world, then I couldn't possibly hate him. At least we could stand each other enough to make babies even if we couldn't do other things together.

Melvin had grown from the loving man that I loved to quite the opposite. My babies were now my sole reason for living. They gave me a purpose to keep on striving even against all odds. They were everything I had, and I was proud that I was a good mother to my kids even though I had no mother to lay an example for me.

I found job at another hotel not far from my apartment. Being the only one I had, I would drop off my kids at my grandmother's house on weekends, so I could go to work. I and Melvin had grown so distant that I doubted if he even noticed me anymore. Sometimes, he would enter the house and brush right past me as though I was nothing more than a piece of furniture. After a while, I stopped dressing up to look nice or even apply make-up. I also stopped buying myself new clothes. All the money I had was going to my kids. It was as though I had given up on life just, so they could live. Deep within me, I knew I looked like crap, but I really didn't care anymore. The fact that other people too would have noticed did nothing to make me stop the self-inflicted punishment. There were times when I wouldn't comb my hair for days although I still made sure my kids looked good every time.

My day was always stressed-filled. Getting home late from work to feed the kids and still spend ample time with them could be very tiring. The down side of it was that I had to go to bed every day knowing full well that I was going to repeat the process the next day. Melvin didn't make things any more pleasant for me as he squandered all his money on drugs.

I got another eviction notice as I was unable to meet up with the payment of the apartment's rent.

108

The landlord made it known that he was tired of my inability to foot the bills and he kicked us out.

The problem then was where we were going to move to. My grandmother's place was out of it because I couldn't imagine going back to the same house where I was raised with my kids. My pride would not just allow me to do that although I knew she was the only one I could run to at that point. She would do anything just to make sure that we were okay.

Melvin was also against moving to my grandmother's place for a different reason entirely. He wanted us to move to his sister's house. I was definitely not taking my kids to his sister's house because I did not like her. I felt that she would take advantage of our present situation to lord over us and I could not take that. I also had the feeling that she knew about the other women that he was messing around with, but she

109

chose not to say anything about it. Therefore, I objected vehemently against the idea.

We eventually got another apartment that was comfortable although smaller to the previous one. The only drawback was that I had to get it in Melvin's name because having had two evictions on my credit report, nobody was going to rent a house to me. I had sunk that low. I was not comfortable with the fact that I had to get the apartment in Melvin's name because it meant that he already had a vital hold on me and my kids. I, however, had no choice.

Moving into the new apartment didn't make anything any better between I and Melvin. We had stopped having sex a long time ago. The kids were the only reason why we were still together.

The kids simply adore him as he often spends time with them. I would often stare longingly at Melvin and the kids as he played games with them and made them laugh. The fact that they

110

had already gotten used to him was enough reason for me to endure living under the same roof with him.

Raising my three kids and working very hard at my job made my life a predictable one. I often had the feeling that I was missing out on all the fun and excitement in life and I knew I had to do something about it if I didn't want to die of boredom. I often feel lonely late at night when my kids were asleep, and Melvin had also gone out as usual.

In my quest to be the best mother for my kids, I had sacrificed a lot of things. For example, since I had my first daughter, I hadn't taken alcohol or even gone clubbing. It was during those lonely nights that I realized that I had missed those things and the excitement that came with them.

One day, finally, I decided to let off some steam by going out for a few drinks. I dropped the kids off at my grandmother's and rushed back home to dress up. Checking myself in the mirror, I could hardly recognize myself as I looked incredibly sexy in the skimpy clothing I had on. I sported a cigarette in that familiar way and off I went to the club.

Getting to the club, I was surprised at the amount of familiar faces that I saw there. Most of those I used to have fun with back then were there, although, like me they had grown. I also saw the most unexpected of all people there – Derrick. The amazing part was that he still remembered who I was. Although, I had seen him around a few times since I got older, we never talked.

I soon started getting the attention of almost all the men at the club. Sitting down there and gulping my drink, I realized that I was still as desirable and appealing as I had always been. Melvin was only too blind to see it. I was getting the attention that he had so much denied me of at the club and even much more.

Not long after I had entered the club, Derrick took his seat beside me and tried to bring back the memories that we've had together. It, however, didn't get to me as I could remember vividly how he abandoned me then. We talked and laughed and drank into the night till I started missing my babies. I couldn't wait to go get them from my Grandmother's place.

Derrick obviously had another plan in mind for the night as he tried to persuade me to follow him home. Although, I was tempted to follow him, I could not bear being apart from my kids any longer. I, however, gave him my number and I rushed to my grandmother's house for my kids.

Derrick must have thought that he was still going to get lucky that night because he called me not long after I had left. I was on phone with him as I entered my grandma's house and we were still catching upon on old times as I got my kids settled into the car. He asked after Melvin and

113

that reminded me of the fact that I had called him earlier to let him know that I would be going out, but he had refused to pick up or even call back. I knew deep within me that he was probably somewhere enjoying himself with another woman.

The more I thought of it, the more infuriated I got with the mere injustice of it. He could mess around with as many women as he wanted but I couldn't. It got to a point that I almost considered giving in to Derrick. I wanted very badly at that moment to do what he had been doing. I wanted to hurt him as much as he had hurt me. Derrick also offered to come over to my place that night, but I declined although I wanted nothing more at that moment than to see him. The only thing that stopped me from giving Derrick the permission to come was that I was scared that Melvin might not stay all night where he went and with that, I ended the conversation with Derrick.

The next morning, I was happy that I hadn't allowed my hormones control me because Melvin had eventually come back home the previous night.

As usual, we didn't say a word to each other until he suddenly broke the icy silence between us. He had seen the bracelet from the club the previous night and he was obviously vexed with the fact that I went clubbing.

He kept on going on and on about how as a mother, I wasn't supposed to go clubbing. He started barraging me with questions and all of a sudden, my once cold and indifferent boyfriend became caring. I was however not deceived because I knew that it was not really about him being caring. He simply wanted to remain in control of my life.

To avoid a full-blown argument, I humored him and answered all his ridiculous questions. I also asked a few questions of my own.

115

Questions like;

Why was it that he could do everything he wanted and still expects me to babysit the kids all the time?

Why were there so many women's contact on his phone, women I didn't know?

Why didn't he love me anymore?

Why weren't we the same happy couple that we started off as?

For the first time since he came back home, I broke down and just cried my heart out.

As usual, Melvin did the best thing he could think of at the moment. He started touching me in a suggestive manner and before long we were kissing passionately. Melvin, being who he was believed that sex was the solution to everything, he believed that sex would make us better and that it would make me forget everything that had gone wrong between us.

Of course, my hormones got the best of me and I ended up succumbing. We closed the door and for the first time in months, we made love. And of course, in my gullibility, I forgot everything in the reverie of our love-making.

From that day onwards, Melvin changed for the better. He was spending more time with us in the house. We were back to being that happy couple again and I almost found it hard to believe that this caring man was really Melvin. We were going out on proper dates as a couple. During that time, I was easily the happiest woman on earth. Because of the excitement that came with having my man back and having my relationship with him restored, I neglected other equally important people in my life. All my attention was focused on Melvin and my kids. I hadn't checked on my grandmother for weeks because things were going on quite well for me.

By the time I realized how wrong my action was, it was almost too late. Grandmother had undergone a breast removal surgery due to the breast cancer that she had, without me being aware. When I found out, I felt stupid and I was disappointed in myself. My grandmother had taken me in when my Mom died and had taken care of me ever since then. She had seen me through my dark times and she loved me even when I found it hard to love myself. Even as an adult, she still cared for me and my little ones. And how exactly had I repaid her? By getting caught up with a man when she needed me most. I disappointed her when I should have stood right by her.

I was angry with myself when I found out about the surgery. My grandmother had been sick for a while and all I could do was focus on my immediate family. The memory of what cancer did to Melvin's mum within a short period of time was still fresh in my mind and I could not imagine the same happening to my grandmother. It was really true that you did not know the worth of what you've got till you realize that you might lose it. My grandmother had always been there for me right from my childhood that I already grown complacent in showing her how much she meant to me. I felt entitled to the love and affection she showed to my kids and me that I didn't even bother trying to do the same for her.

As expected, the newly found love between I and Melvin did not last long. It got to the point where I was convinced that we were both only putting up the show for each other. We continued to pretend to be madly in love with each other to deceive who? I had no idea who we thought we were deceiving. Although he had graduated to dropping me off at work and picking me up after work, it was obvious that we had both ran out of love for each other.

119

Not long after, when it was already obvious that we had both exhausted ourselves of all pretense, we fell back to our old routine – living as roommates. I was tired at this point as it was obvious that our relationship was irredeemable. I had no confidant apart from my grandma and she was the one I ran to for advice. As expected, her advice was that I shouldn't leave Melvin. She however told me that if I and Melvin were not meant to be together, I would know when to quit. While my grandmother expected me to bear it all with the fortitude of a strong woman, she also gave me the option of opting out if it became unbearable.

And indeed, my grandmother was the perfect example of a strong woman. She had suffered a lot of misfortunes, yet she still stood tall with her shoulders held high. It was obvious that she was a survivor as she didn't let anything weigh her down; from losing her daughter who was my

120

mother to battling cancer and beating it. As I was having problems with my relationship, she also had hers with her boyfriend. The only difference between the both of us was that she handled hers way better than I did mine.

Realizing this, I decided to put a stop to Melvin's control over my life. I resolved not to allow him to break me anymore. I was done making him the center of my universe when it was obvious that he was not the man for me.

I started to go to clubs more frequently. I would pay a woman named Janette to babysit my kids while I head out to enjoy myself at the club. It gave me a deep sense of fulfilment knowing that I was also out having fun when Melvin was with women. I derived satisfaction from it, knowing that I was taking revenge on Melvin in my own little way. Going out to clubs gave me a purpose and a reason to be happy.

Unknown to me, when I started clubbing, I had started sinking slowly back into the life that I led as a teenager. I popped Ecstasy pills at every given opportunity although, I restricted it to the bar. I wouldn't take the hard drug at home because of my kids. Cocaine also found its way back into my life and before long I had found myself living the same lifestyle that I had promised myself never to indulge in again.

I was just twenty-two years old, I could not afford to waste my life living like an old woman. The lifestyle I led at night gave me the needed vigor and fervor to perform effectively at work, be a good mother to my kids and pay my bill. At that moment, I believed that I could face virtually anything that life threw at me. Was I really right about this? Were the hard drugs really enough to fill the empty hollow that was in my heart?

CHAPTER SIX

Fast Life and Fast Money

The day after I got back from the club, I made a promise to myself that no matter what happened, I would not be going back into it again. But this promise came too late because it was at that exact time that everything around me began to go downhill. My brother, Jody, went back to jail and it was just crazy. My family depended on me, thinking I was better off than they were. But what they didn't know was that, in the background, I didn't have as much as I presented. I was pretending to have a lifestyle that I didn't have. If I was happy on the outside, I was internally miserable and depressed. My relationship with my kids' father was crashing. Of course, even before now, I had already marked our relationship gone and over. But I didn't let people know on the outside. But this "pretentious" happiness was beginning to be noticed in public and, soon enough, people saw that we were not truly happy as we portrayed ourselves to be— we were struggling like everyone else around us. My brothers didn't understand this. What they wanted was for me to provide for them as well.

It didn't take long for things to begin to fall apart for us. The cocaine I started to use had made things to turn crazier for me. Even though I had tried to, there was no need to pretend everything was alright with me. Moreover, there were a lot of things that were also happening in the family. My grandmother, we soon discovered, had been diagnosed with cancer again. Soon, we made arrangements and took her to the hospital where the doctors removed her breasts entirely. Sometimes, especially whenever I visited the hospital and saw her in her state, I felt like I owed her something important for once in her life, something she would love to see me realize and do. I owed all my brothers, too, I convinced myself. I needed to help them where they needed help. Jody had kids of his own now. I also had my kids to look after. That means, above all, I also needed to support myself and my kids.

By now, I had gradually begun to nurture a wild and nagging thought of making money that eventually paved the way that led me to jail for bank fraud, wired fraud and counterfeit checks. Today, thinking about it, it seemed as if I had always had a way of taking the life right out of me and everyone around me. If not for God and the freedom that he gave to me, I would have no idea where I would be today.

One day, I went to the internet and started researching how to make money real fast. One of the things that popped up and offered to be the quickest way for me to make money was making counterfeit checks. Right there on Google, I diligently studied how to create fake checks.

Once I felt I had learned as much as I would need and that I was ready for it, I decided to give it a try. My thought was that if it didn't work, then I could always try something else. But it worked. The day I made my very first check, I said to myself: "Okay, this looks nice. Let me go and try it out and see." From what my regular work checkbook looked like, I went into BBNT Bank and cashed the check there. The shock I felt when it worked that day was capable of lifting me off the ground, landing me back in a second! Immediately, I used part of the money to buy my brother out of jail. After that, I looked at the success of my first attempt and then said: "I've been struggling, going through all of this. Now is the time for me to use what I have to get what I want."

And I did, without self-control.

The money continued to roll in, and I continued to make them for a few months. I evolved. I got my families members into it, about five of us in total. Once my brother got out of prison, we included him in the business. We became like a small company of criminals— which we were. They called me the Mastermind. We went from city to city, State to State, making counterfeit checks. Once we were done making them and were ready for the real thing, we got some homeless people to cash the checks for us, giving them 100-300 Dollars per check. My cousin Chase was just as much of a hustler as I was and getting him on my team was a power move. I called him up and of course anything with money involved he was ok with it.

There is always a certain euphoria that comes with the immediate possession of money that you would ordinarily not have gotten access to in life. I had that, too. I felt the joys wealth transporting me into a world I had never been before. I was young and rolling in the ease of money to buy as many things I could afford. I finally had the right amount of Dollars to express myself and to pursue the kind of freedom I always wanted for myself and my family.

The irony was that even though I went into making counterfeit checks with the thoughts of meeting the needs of my loved ones, I didn't think about anybody's experience as at that time. All I thought about was that I was having enough money now that was not only capable of making my kids' father happy but also my kids. I made sure they were getting everything that they need.

It didn't take long for us to move into a bigger home that we entirely furnished from the money we were making from the checks. Life was good. Everything was good. I acquired two new trucks— one for myself and another for my kids' father. The money was pouring in, and I realized that we could keep spending as much as we could. Our good life continued for about six months, a time that I was living a split lifestyle so as not to betray my means of comfort. I was practically on the brink of redefining the terms of my existence and those of my loved ones when Fate stroke again.

My nightmare began one morning on my way to Hardees to get my kids something to eat. While I was driving, I noticed that there were two unmarked cars following me, right into the drive-through. As I went through the drive-through, coming back from ordering my food, the police got out of their cars, pulled their guns out and yelled at me to "Get on the ground! Get on the ground!" It was the FBI. They went through the checks with me and, soon enough, my time was up. It was time for me to pay for my sins.

I would have given up everything to make this reality a joke. But, each day that the Court proceedings went on, I realized the mess I had trapped myself in. Even before my arrest, I was very much aware that my way of earning money was illegal and that the day the law caught up with me, I would have to spend several years behind bars.

All of us ended up getting terms in Federal prisons. I pleaded guilty to my charges. There was little to hide, even if I had tried doing so. My little cousin Eli, who was also involved as well, had told them everything that they needed to know. The evidence against us was massive. My brother Jody and my cousin Chase tried everything they could to keep me from going to prison. They told the police I was not involved but of course the FBI knew the truth. The judge sentenced me to eighteen months in prison. There were newspapers articles in regard to our activities. We made news headlines all over the country.

But what was hurting for me the most was the inexplicable pain that I was getting ready to leave my children. I knew I was greedy, wanting more and more money, wanting to help others— which I did. I remember that during the time we were cashing in more checks, I was helping to pay people's bills. But this wasn't all. I also assisted some of them to get their apartments. I had always looked forward to helping someone. And when the opportunity came for me too— even though it was through a criminal route which my beneficiaries were unaware of — I embraced it so much to the point that it nearly ruined my entire life.

The judge gave me ninety days to report myself to the facility that I was to do my time. As at that time, I couldn't decide where my kids would go. And even though I had nowhere in mind, I knew I had to figure out something and do so really fast. But apart from this, my arrest caused a lot of chaos at home, especially with my kid's father. Finally, we decided to go our separate ways. I had always expected this separation. The money was gone. My home was gone. There was no need for us to stay together anymore. He ended up moving in with his aunt. As for me, I wound up at a neighborhood project apartment that I grew up in as a kid, trying to figure out where my kids would go. It was all overwhelming for me.

It was during this time that Tavaris and I met. He was a guy who walked up to me one night and said he knew I was making money and he wanted to get in. I was with Tavaris for some time until the money stopped coming in. He didn't want anything to do with me at all. He saw that "Hey, she's not getting any money at all." But by this time, I found out that I was pregnant with his child, who would turn out to be my fourth daughter. All this while, I was waiting to go for self-surrender to the Federal prison that I was supposed to serve my sentence. When I got pregnant, I relayed the news to Tavaris. I had never seen him so angry like I did that day. His pitch was high as he told me he knew the baby wasn't his, because I just got out of a long relationship with my kids' father.

So, here I was— a convict heavy with a child whose fatherhood was debatable— on my way to the Federal Prison Camp, Alderson. I had tried to be self-sufficient. But now, after my arrest and as I watched my life crumbling before my very eyes, my belief in myself began to disappear, and all of my pride gone. Even though I tried to be strong, every day I woke up, it seemed like everything that my life rotated around was getting worst. But I had no idea that that very day that the FBI caught me, and the judge sentenced me to jail, it was all part of God's work to push on the way to being better.

I ended up getting an extension to when I was supposed to self-surrender to Federal prison. Within those 90 days, I found someone to keep my children. Like everything going wrong in my life, my plans for my kids didn't go well, too. When I was in prison, I received news that my kids were being abused and put into things they shouldn't have been put through. I needed to act fast. I contacted my cousin, Lashae, to go to the person who had my kids and retrieve them through the custody forms that I submitted before my incarceration. Before she got them, they were fine. I wanted to make sure that by the time I was getting out of jail, my kids would be alright. Since I had wanted to pay for the wrongs that I did alone, no one needed to tell me that my innocent kids would also suffer along with me. When I think back on my life, I imagine what it felt like to have lived a part of my childhood having a mother in jail— the batteries, the bruising knowledge and the humiliation of living with it— I felt so sorry for my kids for all they went through.

I had regrets. Great ones. In my cell, my emotions somersaulted between shame, disgust, and disappointment with myself and then, suddenly, I would withdraw into that same self to find shelter from my guilt. I knew I had done wrong, terribly so. But I could never paint myself in prison in a clear picture of forgiveness.

I ended up finishing my sentence and also giving birth to my daughter. Now, I need to state here that my eighteen-month sentence didn't exactly turn out to be eighteen months. At this time, I understood how the renewal of our minds is capable of changing us into better people. And as unoriginal as this may sound, my renewal began when I met Christ in prison.

While I was in prison, I met a group of excellent women who influenced me into thinking more positively about life. I began to accept the fact that there was still a beautiful journey ahead for me to take and that all that I had been through and had done were part of my preparation for that journey.

135

Along with these women, I developed a fresh interest in church. There was this little choir we had. It was in it that I began to sing in the church and enjoyed doing so. I've always told people that I was pretty sure that my prison experience was what drew me closer to God. It became so bright that I needed to be isolated for me to hear what it was that God was trying to tell me and to for me to see and know what direction he wanted me to go in. At first, it sounded crazy, but that was what happened. Of all the stupidest things I had done in my entire life until that moment, it took me going to prison to finally realize that there were so much better things for me beside the lifestyle that I was living.

After I spent the six months of my incarceration instead of eighteen months, I came home. When I went out of prison, I went to the halfway house. It never occurred to me to go back to Columbia, South Carolina. Instead, as if a force beyond my control was guiding me, I went somewhere in South Carolina where there were women who were employees in the halfway house there. Some of them were case workers while others were just some regular employees. They took me under their wings, encouraged me to do better and assisted me in finding a job. If I had thought they had done enough for me, I was wrong. They didn't stop there. They went further to collect money, put down in security deposit into an apartment so that I could get my children back upon being released from prison.

I found a church home in South Carolina. I was working and going to church. Even the women in the church were always around to tend to my children whenever I was at work. The person I remember today among them the most was Miss Brigitte. Brigitte's cousin and I were incarcerated together in FPC, Alderson. It was from there that she and I began to know each other.

137

When I started working, Brigitte would always be there to attend to my children. She would pick my children up in the morning and take them to school while I was at the halfway house and then when I got to work; she would pick them up from school and bring them back to her place. This benevolence went on for months. The rest of my stay at the halfway house took me another year which, altogether, completed my eighteen-month sentence. By now, this meant that I had spent six months in incarceration in Alderson Federal Prison and then the twelve months in the halfway house where Miss Brigitte assisted with making sure that I would get back on track.

After my prison experience, I began to nurture myself to put everything in my past behind me. I made sure I put in the past all the people I knew before who were not with me at this moment; these people were in my former life. Being in a new environment with new people seemed like

138

God putting people around me— to encourage me, to push me to greater heights and to help me discover myself daily. There were no more drugs. I didn't even have the desire to smoke cigarettes. I also had no cravings for liquor. It was merely me and my God, and that's all the equation that mattered at that time. And then there were the people that he sent to shower love on my children and me. They showered me with so much genuine attention and love that I thought, "I don't deserve this!"

I was passing through a phase in my life that marked the end of the relationship between my children's father and me. Now, I had a fourth child by Tavaris. Of course, he wasn't there when she was born. She didn't even know who he was.

But my life continued.

I was now a single mother with four children, freshly released from prison. I got a fresh start in a new city where I didn't know anyone. But God,

139

in his mercies, provided for me. He made sure that he ordered my steps the moment that I stepped out of prison. Everything was mapped out for me already. I got a place to stay, a job working at a hotel and all my four beautiful children were in my custody. I was determined more than ever not to lay back. I could only go up from there. There was no more self-pity. I was using my past to keep me in a safe situation. I was focused, always waking up daily in the morning to pray and ask God to guide me and to help me and my children.

Even though I sometimes felt lost, being a single mother, I knew that God was holding my hands through the darkness and that at the end of it all, I would be just fine— in the light.

CHAPTER SEVEN

Losing It All

So far, my experiences had taught me that the moment we decide to do the right thing and to live a lifestyle that doesn't consist of doing wrong, is the exact moment that the devil, too, chooses to make sure we do exactly the opposite.

When I got out of jail and settled into a new home together with my four girls, I met another guy who proved to me that I was not yet as wiser as I thought I was. His name was Jamario. Because I was a single mother, he presented himself to be the right man for me, and I believed him. Jamario came with the right words and attitude. He was always there to assist me with the bills when we started dating. Few weeks into our relationship, he finally met my children. His intentions were genuine, or so I thought.

Jamario and I dated for about five months before I discovered that I was pregnant again with my fifth child. Thinking about it now, I could not help getting mad at myself all over again. I was a very fertile woman with four children who didn't think it foolish to have unprotected sex with a man who wasn't her husband. I had made a promise to God that I was going to be different. Because I reneged on my words, I felt embarrassed, humiliated and disgusted with myself.

Once, I tried to have an abortion, but it was already too late for me to do that because I was already three and a half months in. According to my first doctor, I was not just carrying a child, but twins! How could I reveal my pregnancy to my pastor, my family and everyone who expected me to stay on the right path? How could I be so stupid?

I finally got the courage to inform my pastor about my pregnancy. Her reaction was entirely contrary to what I expected from her. Instead of being angry and disappointed with me, she calmly took the time to remind me that I was a human being, incapable of perfections and that God, who is perfect and always merciful, is always ready to forgive us whenever we must have messed up along the way. Unlike man, he doesn't hold grudges or mistreat us when we do something that isn't pleasing to him.

I knew I had made a lot of mistakes and had disappointed not only myself but also God and my children. I had to get myself back to that place where nothing else mattered except God. I noticed that when Jamario and I started dating, I was no longer praying as I should. Instead, I went back to smoking cigarettes. When it dawned on me that I was spending the most critical part of my life with someone who shouldn't be there in the beginning, I began to entertain the thought of ridding my life and my children's life of Jamario's presence.

One night, I went into my room and prayed fervently to God, asking him to restore me to the person I became after my prison experience. I knew that getting rid of Jamario would mean I would have to raise my children alone again, without any external help. But before he came into my life through a path that I naïvely opened to him, I was doing just fine alone. And God did not forsake me either. I was a single parent with the mighty presence of God with me.

My resolution to drive Jamario away became firmer when one day I found out that he was using cocaine. That day, I swore that I was neither going back that path nor would I allow him to ruin my children for me. My senses told me that with a man like him in the house, my girls were potential victims of abuse. I had to do something very fast not just for myself but also for their safety.

One fine, Monday evening after I picked my girls up from Mrs. Bridgette, I returned home and found Jamario in the living room, passed out with bottles of liquor scattered everywhere. I went to where he was lying on the sofa and kicked him back to reality. Once he regained consciousness, I asked him to go inside the bedroom, get his things and leave my house immediately.

I have always justified my act of sending Jamario as the best thing to do at that time. I knew his lifestyle was the same lifestyle that led me right into jail in the past, and I did not need anyone to remind me of the consequences of going that way again. The thoughts of what my girls passed through without me and the experiences I had in prison were still vivid in my memories. I didn't need a man to bring me down again.

When Jamario and I started seeing each other, he wasn't living with me. But he was always at my place until he accumulated his clothes there. His

145

x-box game was also at my place. The day he packed his things and left, I was finally alone with my children, and I loved the feeling of the new peace that momentarily came with his departure. Even though I was pregnant with his children, I told Jamario to go and never return or call me again. I was truly prepared to move on, alone with my girls and my God who was always there for me, even when I was still doing things that were contrary to what he would have wanted of me.

Several months had come and gone, and I still didn't hear from Jamario. I had thought he would have, at least, try to initiate a kind of contact, anyway that was possible for him to do. But when he didn't contact me again, I wasn't upset with him. I was the one who asked him to leave, and never to return or call me again. Jamario was merely following my orders. But not for long.

When it was time for me to give birth to the twins, just when I was finally determined to do without

146

him, Jamario called me again. He lamented how much he had always wanted to be in the girls' life, but he couldn't due to his wrong lifestyle. But he would love to make reparations to us, especially now that I would be given birth to his daughters— he wanted to be present in their life above anything else. I listened to the tempo of his voice over the line as he talked about how much he had changed his life around. He sounded genuine, and I believed him once again.

I gave Jamario permission to be there with me when I gave birth to our daughters. Since the C-section was a scheduled one, I knew the exact time to give him to be at the hospital. But on the morning of my surgery, I had no one by my side except Debra. She was a friend I met when I moved to Florence, and we instantly became very close. Debra was also there with me during the whole time I was pregnant.

147

Once the doctors put me on the monitor to check the heartbeats of the baby, they discovered that I had only one baby alive inside. Jamario still hadn't shown up. I later got to know he came to the hospital through the events that his coming orchestrated.

When Jamario arrived at the hospital, at last, I was already in surgery, the doctors trying to make sure that my baby and I survived. Instead of Jamario to stay with me, he went ahead to retrieve my car keys from my bag in the room and left. I didn't realize my car wasn't in the parking lot nor did I realize he was even there until I recovered. When I got back into my room, a call came through to me from jail. It was Jamario, calling to tell me that he got pulled over for drunk driving. My God! Here I was in the hospital; I had just lost one baby and given birth to another and here was there father, eternally irresponsible, calling to tell me he was in jail.

I now had five daughters to care for, and it was evident that Jamario would not be a good father figure to them. He had proved this right on the very first day I was giving birth to his own daughters.

After the delivery, I couldn't bring my thoughts together. The realization that I had just lost a child shredded me inside. When I began purchasing things before the delivery, I did so in double— for both girls. But my consolation from grief came when I considered the place of God in everything. If he saw it fit to make my daughter an angel— my angel— then I had no right whatsoever to question his will. I named the girls Aaliyah and Jaliyah. Jaliyah came out so healthy and with so much personality that seemed to say it was enough for her and her sister. Right from their birth, I so firmly believed that my two girls, the one who left and the one who stayed, were, together, another starting point of my redemption.

God would use them and my other four girls to uplift me and make my dreams and goals soar into life.

I left the hospital penniless and without a car. The fact that it was another man who made it happened— a man who once tried to ruin my life, a man who didn't even get the chance to see his daughters while he was in jail— made me angrier with myself.

A week after I left the hospital, I heard a knock at the door. When I opened it, I found Jamario on the terrace, smiling as if the world sent him to save me. He was here to see his daughters, he said. I let him know there was only one of them who survived. When he spoke, his speech was slurred, and he could barely stand. Inside the house, the smell of alcohol on his body unsettled me so much that I nearly ordered him to get out of my house for the second time. But I restrained myself. He attempted to hold Jaliyah, but I stopped him. Only an insane mother would allow a drunken father to hold her child. And I wasn't insane.

When I stopped Jamario from holding Jaliyah, he asked if only I would allow him to shower, he would leave immediately. Then, my other children were in their rooms playing. I allowed Jamario to go into my bathroom and shower. I was seething inside, still wondering what he was doing in my house, in my life. How did I get here? I kept asking myself these questions when my second daughter came running into the living room, panting. When I asked her what the problem was, she told me, her hands pointing in the direction of my bathroom, that Jamario asked her to get in the shower with him. That was it! Right there, whatever knot that had been holding my anger in check was let loose, and I lost my mind! I literally took everything I could grab and threw at him, right inside the bathroom.

151

Jamario ran out of my house, still in his drunk state, with no shoes or shirt on. How could he be so insensitive to try something as absurd and abusive as this, after all my children had already been through? Once Jamario left the house, I immediately packed all of our clothes up, left all the furniture behind and headed back to Columbia SC where I said I would never return. I was a single mother with five children and with no place to live again. This must surely be the definition of loss.

I arrived in Columbia SC and moved in with my cousin, Tashamber. Her mother lived with her as well as her three children. I knew I wouldn't be there for long because I also had five children. But this wasn't the only reason. Tashamber was very manipulative and deceitful as well as her best friend. I wasn't used to living with anyone. I stayed with Tashamber and her family for about a week and a half and then moved into my own place.

The man who rented to me knew I was struggling. At last, he allowed me to keep the $500 I had. I owed that man my starting out. We only needed a place to lay our heads, and he helped with what I had. I move in.

The girls and I lived directly across from Tashamber, and I thought, at first, it was cool. I had no furniture in the home because I left everything behind after the incidence with Jamario. To survive, I decided to find a job as soon as possible so as to pay the landlord.

Jaliyah was three weeks old when I applied for government assistance to assist with getting a welfare check as well as food stamps. I found a job making $8.25 an hour, and I knew it wasn't much. Neither my five children nor I would be able to survive off of this.

153

It was around this time that I also began to lose interest in meeting any man again. I already resolved within me that men were my downfall. I started focusing on rebuilding my life and making sure I was always able to provide for my girls. My aunt, Tashamber's mom, volunteered to keep my children to let me put my energy into doing other things. I gladly accepted her offer.

Tashamber and I were hanging out one night when I met Barkee. He wasn't exactly someone new to me. We went to the same school together. He and I exchanged contacts. I did nothing to impress him or to hide any secret from him. Even though things were rough with me as a single mother, I was proud of my life; I was prouder of my girls. I told Barkee I had five children; the last was a newborn. He was very attentive as I spoke about them one after the other, and by the time we had said goodbye, I noticed that there was something markedly different about him that attracted me. It wasn't like I was ready to jump into a relationship or anything of that nature after what I had gone through. I didn't think of that.

I also wasn't definitely going to bring another man around my girls after what Jamario did. With Barkee, I was quite comfortable keeping our friendship just what it was— friendship.

Barkee and I talked on the phone daily and every little chance we had, he took me out to lunch and dinner. Even though he was yet to meet any of my girls, he would buy gifts and send to them through me.

I had built a wall up around my heart, scared to love again. Barkee and I didn't get too far when I started to develop contempt for our friendship. Even though I had a newborn baby and four other children, he didn't allow that to bother him.

A few months later I invited Barkee home for breakfast. He was a very busy man who worked

Monday through Friday third shift, which made him available only on weekends. But he came. My baby, Jaliyah, felt an instant attachment to Barkee and soon grew to love him. In fact, her first words were "Daddy," and they were directed at him.

Barkee paid all of my bills while I was on a fixed budget and what I loved and respected about him was the way he made it his duty to respect the changes I wanted in my life. We both knew he wasn't perfect. But, I could clearly see the efforts he was putting each day into trying to impress my girls and to treat me like a queen. It was something that my family never experienced before. Barkee respected my girls and called each one of them "Princess."

But there was something about Barkee that I disliked— his habitual clubbing and smoking of weed. He knew my aversion to this lifestyle. When he discovered this, he made it a rule never to come around my children that way. One day, during one of the several discussions I had with him about goals, I told him I didn't like his smoking and clubbing habit, and I couldn't bring him anymore around my children while he was high on weed. Right there, Barkee vowed to stopped smoking weed altogether and told me: "If that's what it takes to show you I love you and the kids, consider it done!" And it was done. Just like that!

There were many things that he did and undid in his attempts to prove to me how much he was willing to sacrifice so as to be able to love us unconditionally. And he did this despite the brokenness I had experienced in my life.

The best part about Barkee was that he didn't want sex from me. He had shown me that he was willing to wait as long as I would have him wait. I found this to be very strange. Every man I had dealt with in the past wanted sex from me. But

157

here was Barkee teaching me that all men could not be the same— and would never be.

Despite Barkee's gestures of love and care, I was still scared to love again. My children were growing to love him. It was in Jaliyah's life that Barkee solidified his intentions. Knowing she didn't have her father's presence in her life, he made sure he did for her everything a father would do— since from when she was just three months old. He brought all the pampers, milk, wipes, put her to sleep, fed her, played with her daily and didn't miss a single doctor's visit. He was also around on her birthday.

Two years had passed since Barkee, and I met, and he was still right there through everything. During this two year-time-frame, I briefly lost custody of my children due to a problem I had with my cousins. It was crazy to me because it was a cousin from my fathers side and one from my mothers side that conspired together to have my children removed from me. My mental health past became an issue and the fact that I was starting over didnt help the situation. When my girls were taken from me, I tried to commit suicide again. I was literally messed up in every way possible. My past mistakes suddenly came back to torment me. I hated myself and regretted every single decision I had made in the past.

Many nights during my trying times, I cried to God to help me. I cried to him like the Psalmist: "Take hold of your shield and stand up for my help" (Psalms 35:2). I discovered something about God long ago. He is always there to stand up and defend the honor of those who are fighting battles each day. He takes the place of their husband, and whenever he's allowed to, he readily becomes a father to the fatherless children. I tasted this grace before and knew that it was what had kept me alive so far. After all, I had gone through, to be alive and be able to write my story is nothing short of grace. I also believe it was God who gave Barkee to me when I really needed him.

Barkee, without demanding anything in return, kept pushing me to do better, to want better and to be better. While I was so broken, scared to love again, he was right there through it all.

My biggest worry was that my kids' father wasn't doing anything for them. The anger I felt each time I thought about that made me become mean to Barkee. But Barkee refused to be shaken. Instead, he worshipped and loved the ground my kids and I walked on. He made it look like it was about me, about the girls, and not about him. Gradually, he succeeded in redefining every other assumption I had about men along the years.

I would never wish anyone the pains of going through the stress, pains, and occasional disappointments of child custody battle. Sometimes at night, bouts of depression came over me— the loneliness and grief over losing my girls were getting too much to contain. All of a sudden, I realized how hard and frightening my life had become.

Everything I had tried to do right had gone wrong entirely. I had been into relationships that seemed to end even before they begin. I had children waiting for me somewhere to gather them into my arms. My family members had put a wound on me that I was sure was going to be on me for a long time. I was going through life with a weight that was far beyond my frame and energy, and I was reaching my breaking point.

But, God wasn't done with me yet.

There were these twins Brenda and Brelay who were Gods gift to me. They took my children in when DSS removed them from me and didn't treat them different than their own. These twins I have always called my aunts but they are really close friends of my family. Lashaes mother

161

happens to be one of them. My children could not have been placed in a better environment than with them.

During the period of my struggles to take back my children, Barkee went to every psychiatric visit with me, visited my children with me as well as helped me move into a new place to get them back. If my family had failed me, he proved to me that I didn't only have God on my side, but I also had him right in my corner. To be honest, Barkee, Lashae, Brenda and Brelay were all I had besides God. They became my circle of support and pushed me daily.

Five weeks later, I got my children back, and I was ready to move again. Out of all the hell I was going through none of my childrens fathers tried getting their children. My oldest three girls father had fell off of Earth completely, my disabled daughters family didn't even know what my daughter looked like because they were waiting on blood test results and of course Jaliyah dad was never getting the opportunity to be around her after what he had done. I settled in Charlotte, NC. And Barkee was coming with me.

CHAPTER EIGHT

All Things Were Working Out For My Good

It is said that each person we meet in life serves either one of these two purposes: to be a blessing or a lesson. I am afraid to say that so far, going by my story, all the men I had met had been a lesson to me.

If you are like me, a woman who had fallen in and out of extreme and staggering relationships with the wrong men, after going through that hamster wheel of emotional death, you would have by now become more careful than ever whenever you get the chance to meet some new man in your life. You would be focused on finding someone who would love and need you for the right reasons, without that constant emotional instability, tendencies to lie, explosive tempers and expectations that are too real to be real to both partners. But the hunger for love goes beyond human reasoning. It is the way we are wired as humans. There is absolutely no shame in being optimistic about love, desiring something positive or being naturally responsive to people in a way that shows you care. This internalized or nurtured way in our daily interactions with people does not change even if there are disappointments on the long run. I had been in different relationships with so many men in my life that went wrong and then just when I thought I had given up and wanted nothing to do with a man, there would be someone out there who would come out from nowhere to prove me wrong. I had already told the story of Barkee in the previous chapter and how he had dispelled me of all the previous thoughts I had of men that were not so encouraging. Barkee stood by me, wanting nothing but giving everything. He was there, in the light and in the shadows, just waiting for me to

165

reach out to him, and he was with me, like an angel.

When I moved to Charlotte, NC, Barkee was there with me, too. Even though I had tried my best to cater for my children alone as a single mother, I already knew that the only way for me to successfully give my daughters the life they would be proud of was to find the right person for me that would be ready to sync his energy with mine and be with them. I needed a man who would be proactive as a problem-solver, and always on the ready to transform his thoughts into substantial things.

Most nights, I stayed awake, asking myself if Barkee was the right man for me and my daughters. Because of my daughters, I questioned each man that I had encountered so far in my life. I realized that I wasn't alone now, and that it wasn't about me anymore. I had never suppressed my subconscious in doubting any man I met. I needed to be sure at first before I would do anything that might cause harm to me and my daughters again.

Even though I was in love with Barkee, I could not display my love for him whenever there were people around us. I was afraid of public judgment, thinking that people would look at me differently. My reason was that I had been in a very long relationship with the father of my first three kids. What would people say by the time they discovered that I was in another relationship with another man again? These questions that took people's validation of me to be more important than when I had personally validated myself was something I had learned to stop a long time ago. I was perfectly aware that Barkee loved and respected my advice and opinion. He was always trying to understand my dreams and ambitions while also becoming more concerned with my self-identity than I was.

167

Each time I looked Barkee over whenever we were together, I could tell that his wanting me in his own life, too, went far behind sex. He was simply in love with me as well. Sometimes, whenever we were at the house, he and I would have conversations about what I wanted in life. He never made it about him, but about me. I tried to go beyond his concerns for me to see if maybe there might just be some selfish reasons lurking therein. In my previous relationships, the men were altruistic at first; they would always show they care, until just when I had surrendered myself to them that their true nature would begin to come to the surface. But, with Barkee, no matter how hard I tried to doubt his love and intentions, I always failed.

Barkee would always ask me what I thought my kids would want and what made me feel so special. This was all new and exciting to me. I know I had spent a greater part of the last chapter writing about Barkee. And I am still doing that, too, here. It was because I was at a stage in my life where I thought I would be giving up on so many things that really mattered to me that Barkee emerged, proving to be of such monumental help to me and my children. I never had a man in my life that put my kids first before anything, as if they were his own. Except Barkee!

But I knew if I was to have any relationship with Barkee, it would not go far. As good as he had proven to be, he was not the type of men I knew before who would go to church or pray. After all the hell I had been through, after seeing how much God had been there for me, despite of my moments of considerable weakness and failures, I knew I needed a partner who would pray with me. I was at a point in my life that I needed more than just financial provision. At the moment, it seemed that that was all Barkee could give, if I let him into my life totally. So, I delayed a bit, and Barkee still refused to move.

It didn't take long for me to find a job when we settled down in Charlotte, NC. This was after I got my kids back with me. Barkee would sit in the hotel I was working at and keep them for me while I worked. Even without him saying it, I knew he so much wanted this job to work as much as I did. He knew how many times I had moved from one job to the other due to how my life had turned out to be.

I was new in Charlotte and didn't know anyone in the city. Because of this, Barkee was always in my corner all the way to keep me company and to prevent me from pangs of loneliness. He and I were still not having sex because we had had conversations where I told him I was the least interested in sleeping with a man again and all I was crazed about was to try to have a new life for me and my kids. The day we had this conversation, I expected him to be disappointed and, maybe, stopped coming around, since he wouldn't be having what he had initially wanted to have. But Barkee wasn't disappointed a bit. In fact, he waited for me until I was ready to have sex with him.

Most days during the night, we would have our usual conversations where Barkee would talk about him wanting me to do what I think was the best for me. His response was: "When I said, 'I love you,' I didn't just say that, so I could get under your clothes. I love you because you are you. If I have to wait for years, then I will wait on you." His understanding and calm attitude in place where I expected misunderstanding and harshness were too surreal to be true. But that was Barkee. He was not the type to force me or any woman to have sex with him. He did not nag me about it neither did he begin to display strange behaviors because of my rejection of his needs.

Deep down, I knew that Barkee was a man with needs and I was also a woman with needs. Even then, I knew that a man in love is a complex person, so complex that he might be prompted by his emotions to act so feminine. Sometimes, I stepped back and think of him, trying to fully get to know him not principally as a man, but as a human being in love with me; a man who, like all other men out there, would be on fire and subjected to emotion, passion, doubts about their feelings and even ecstasy. I was immensely grateful that he could be all of this and yet chose to make a commitment to me. But I wanted to do the right thing. I wanted to offer him myself at the right time. Even though he did not go to church or pray as I would have him do, Barkee wanted me to live a life that was pleasing to God. As long as it made me happy, he was okay with it.

But beyond his needs for a sexual outlet, which never brought problems between us, Barkee never failed to let me know for once how I was his future wife! At first, I didn't believe he knew what he was talking about and I started to believe that he was just crazy and in love.

When I saw that we were not having sex and yet Barkee was still around me and talking about me being his wife, I started to think that he wanted something else from me. Gradually, I pushed him away until he moved back home to Columbia SC. Within me, I was perfectly sure that I didn't mean to send him away because I truly needed him around me.

Most men I had met were afraid of commitment and even when they did commit in the end, they always loved to control the direction of our relationship. But in Barkee, I found a man who was not only ready to commit to me (and had already begun to do so) but was also willing to love my children as if they were his own. He loved me. He was willing to give up the places and

173

everything he knew before I came into his life just to start over with me. But I pushed him away! I think, sometimes, we experience love that's so magnificent that we are afraid to open our heart to it. I experienced the same thing with Barkee.

When Barkee left Charlotte, NC, I felt sick being away from him. He was my best friend whom I could tell anything and not be afraid that I would be judged. Whenever we talked, he would try to actually listen to me without faking it. I began to recollect all the talks we had about goals in life and how I had successfully made him to begin praying with me. Barkee and I were building something together, but I was afraid to take things further with him because I wasn't his wife yet. He wanted something greater and so did I.

Deep down, I knew that he was the man for me and I wanted to be with him forever. But I was trying my best to be patient, to learn how to wait for the right time.

I would never understand how God works, and neither have I tried to. All my life, since the day I encountered God all those years in prison, I had learned to give way and let God do his thing. I believe that God knows the deepest thoughts we have within us and if they are for good, He creates a miracle that would have us laughing in the end. During the days I was missing and yearning for Barkee, he came back to me from nowhere and with a ring! He asked me a question that I had waited my entire life to hear: "Will you marry me?"

I said yes, with tears in my eyes.

I knew this was God at work, forever looking after his own. He was the One who had sent Barkee to me and brought us to this defining moment in our lives. After three men who had appeared and disappeared out of my life, after five children to look after as a single mother, after a prison sentence that nearly made me feel I had lost my place in the world, God found me and now, it was time for a wedding!

We set the date for September 19, 2015. I believed the children were more excited than I was. They had known me with Barkee and had already created a place in their beautiful and innocent hearts for him as a father. I believed that they were fully aware of the men that had come in and out of my life and how much I had endured. But, above all, I was the one who owed the greatest duty to them: find them a man they could call "Father." And what better than Barkee!

My excitement to be Barkee's wife was unabashed. I was fully ready to be identified with him. He was my friend. He was my love. He was the only constant thing that remained when the friends and family I had looked up to failed me and departed from my life. Barkee and I set goals in the beginning and that one goal that I always looked forward to achieving was to build a

176

relationship with God. There were days that my life got so busy and stressful that I got bogged down and forgot about God. He knew I was imperfect, that I made mistakes and all that made me was nothing but human, someone He, out of love, created and swore to love and provide for. It was this sheer love that God had and still has for me and my children that made him take me on the process that led to this moment. He had challenged me and made me to be fully prepared for the future he was planning for me. This happened even when I was too weak to completely trust in him and when I had wavered. But just as the Bible said in Romans 5:8, that "God shows his love for us in that while we were still sinners, Christ died for us," God had shown me his love and abundant grace in the moments that I felt I had failed him the most.

Barkee and I knew that in spite of our past, our God had greater plans for us and that his love for

177

us was always meant to be an ongoing act. Because of this knowledge, we were more than determined to live the life he set before us, putting him first in all that we would do. I was about to become a Mrs. Faust and I was excited about it. When I broke the news that Barkee and I were getting married, there were many who tried to talk me out of it. We both came from the hood and had lived a life that wasn't so pleasing to anyone. But God is a God of forgiveness and I wanted to show my friends and family how happy I could be.

I was undeterred when I was advised against marrying Barkee. I loved him, and he loved me, and I felt in my spirit that this was who God had picked out to be perfect for me.

Besides, I knew the power of prayer. Due to that, I began to cover Barkee in prayer daily. My action was spurred by the words in the Bible which says: "For the unbelieving husband has been sanctified through his wife, and the unbelieving wife has been sanctified through her believing husband. Otherwise your children would be unclean, but as it is, they are holy" (1 Corinthians 7:14).

I believed, and with my belief, I knew what God could do. Barkee and I started to attend church and prayed daily together. Our combined faith was enough to tear down any strongholds or generational curses. There was a task set before us, but I knew that God's plans for me, for Barkee and for my children were for all of us to prosper. I held on to that belief as if I had nothing else to hold on to. And, indeed, I had nothing!

God Himself had affirmed His good intentions for us when He said, "For I know the plans I have for you declares the Lord, plans to prosper you and not harm you, plans to give you hope and a future" (Jeremiah 29:11). I knew this to be true. The day I agreed to become Barkee's wife, I knew I was walking not just into marriage but also into something greater than our own doing,

179

something whose actualization neither Barkee nor I could have projected. God, who had promised us a future, made sure that we walked into it in high hopes, never afraid to trust in his plans and all the things He had in store for us and our children. It was God who had pulled me into his light out of the great darkness I was living, that life of sin that separated me not just from him but also from my loved ones. He had shown to me and my children times without number that everything he had taken us through, my prison sentence, the period my kids lived without me, were all parts of His goal to take us through life with hope and happiness.

I had always believed in God. And whatever He deemed fit, my husband and I believed and were glad.

CHAPTER NINE

Double for Your Trouble

Barkee and I were married on September 19, 2015. This wouldn't go without me saying that it was one of the best and happiest days of my entire life. Most of my family members and friends I had not seen for some time came from far and near to witness as we become one. It was amazing!

But my greatest source of joy was not the wedding itself. It was my five amazing children who were thoughtful enough to say that September 19th was the first time in a long time they saw me being so truly happy. They were right. I knew so, too. For many years before I met Barkee, I was never truly a happy woman. My children were the only reason for my happiness and I was (still am) grateful that God deemed it out of his abundant grace to bless my life with them.

Before you get to the end of this story, there are few things that I feel are important to point out to you. Everything I had gone through in my life wasn't easy for me. I would be lying to you if I said I didn't want to give up at some point. In fact, there were days I was so discouraged that I thought of giving up totally.

I tried everything I could to cope with life in general and to see that my kids were happy. I tried to protect them from the darkness that seemed to constantly engulf me. But the more I tried, the more it became apparent that nothing was working out. I could not do it alone. This continued until I met Jesus.

It always feels good to belong to a God who makes your happiness his ultimate priority. He had advised us in Luke 6:23 to "Rejoice in that day, and leap for joy, for, behold, your reward is in heaven." My joy today comes from the knowledge that I am a beneficiary 1) of God's forgiveness of sins, 2) a fellowship with him, 3) and his eternal presence in my life whenever it seems that things are not working out according to my expectations. This knowledge also gives me the courage to "be strong in the Lord and the in the strength of His might" (Ephesians 6:10).

When I finally gave God a true and a powerful 'Yes!" when I decided that no matter what would happen, no matter the challenges in my life, I was going to follow Jesus and that's all that matters. I had joy in knowing my troubles would not last always. I knew the process wasn't going to be easy. But when I stopped focusing on how big my problems were and began to focus on God and how big of a Problem Solver he could be, things began to look different. Gradually, I watched as my life began to take the shape I had always wanted it to take. I was bathing in the overflowing

183

favor of God. But I had to surrender and forget about a lot of things bothering me. I did, and God didn't forsake me, not even for once!

I lost my mother when I was only four years old. As I grew up, I embraced a life of lies, crime and deceit. I became addicted to drugs which I used daily. I became addicted to alcohol, which I made sure I had until I drunk myself into a slump. I have lost count of the number of men I had slept with. I had gone to prison. I had lost all my children at some point in my life due to some circumstances that my choices, priorities, and mistakes in life necessitated. I had attempted suicide on several occasions. I had gone through a point in my life where I knew nothing but loneliness. I had lost touch with my family and friends.

That was my past.

But in all I had gone through, I was walking in grace. Giving my life to the Lord was the best thing that could have happened to me. Things still get rough and I still go through tough times. But as I sit here and write this, in all honesty, I am telling you that you can go to bed one day and still wake up another the next. You have the blessing of life. God keeps his promises and it is up to us to trust him.

Sometimes all I have when I have nothing is my faith in God to keep me through each passing day. I advise you to get into a relationship with God. Do not lean on your own understanding. I advise you to surrender to him. Some trials come but if we hold on to God's unchanging hand, he is there to lead and guide us daily.

When Barkee and I got married, we had some goals that we set and believed God to help us achieve them. Although I had briefly outlined some of them in the previous chapter, let me reemphasize them fully here.

The first goal we set was to keep God at the center of everything we do. We realized that we can't go into a single battle alone without God on our side. We hope to focus our faith in God and to look up to him because, as Paul made it clear in Ephesians 3:20, it is "… him who is able to do far more abundantly than all that we ask or think…"

The second goal was to not look back on our past but to move forward in God. If you observe some of my shortcomings above, if I had dwelled on them, I would have deemed myself unworthy of God's grace. That would be what the devil would want me to think, and by doing so, I would continue to wallow in my sins. Thank God for calling us to knowledge and truth, I realized that God was always expecting me to return into forgiveness. It is just like in the Parable of the Parable Son narrated by Jesus in Luke 15:11-32, where the loving father of the erring son was always waiting for him all through the years of his wandering to return home into his arms, into a fatherly forgiveness. I knew that God was a merciful God who is always calling us into forgiveness and salvation. Barkee and I decided not to focus on our past but, instead, to look forward to God.

The third goal was to become business owners. This was so that we could have a steady and reliable source of income.

The fourth goal was to get our credit repaired and then to become homeowners, which also happened to be the last goal we set for the first five years of marriage.

These were the goals we wanted to accomplish before the fifth year of our marriage. I am happy to say that we have been successful in achieving each of them and our faith in God still remained the same. We had learned to trust him when we decided to set those goals and God had proven to us that he can be trusted. We still continue to trust in him to this day before we set any goal for ourselves.

I don't know what you have done in your life and, let' say, I don't really care to know. All I care to tell you is that if you remain in God and keep him first in everything you do, there are always benefits in carrying the DNA of God. Remember you are his reflection, his child, and he is always there waiting for you, ready to take care of you. All he wants from you is that, you should believe in him and know that he is a God who keeps his word.

Take Abraham, for example. Romans 4 says he was justified and saved because of his faith and not because of his works. It was through this faith that Abraham obtained a promise from God:

"For the promise to Abraham and his offspring that he would be the heir of the world did not come through the law but through the righteousness of his faith" (vs. 13).

This means that your blessings, your happiness, your prosperity and your victory rest on the stronghold of your faith in God who gives us the

188

grace to believe in him. The Bible is replete with stories and references of men and women who had believed in God and were exposed to his glory and marveled by his absolute readiness to honor those who believe in him.

Hebrews 11 says that Abraham followed God even though he was not sure where he was going. If you read the story of Abraham, it should let you know that God is faithful, and we can put our trust in him. This is one of the stories that keep me going strong in spite of my past experiences.

Sometimes, I'm not sure where God will take me next. But because I have faith in his plans for me, which are plans "for welfare and not for evil, to give you a future and a hope," (Jeremiah 29:11), I hold on to him, because God, forever the great fulfiller of promises, will not allowed his hands to come off of me yet. I have had a really tough life. But I have been through the dark times with the light of God's promises and kindness with me. He always knows the ways and manners of his actions and even though they are hard for me to understand, I simply try to "act justly and to love mercy and to walk humbly with my God" (Micah 6:8).

I have learned to wait on the Lord and to do things according to his will. I am confident that he establishes the steps of those who look up to him for direction. Sometimes, this can be difficult to do and at other times, it seems it seems as if God is simply not there, neither is he listening or answering our cry for help and guidance. But this, too, takes faith, to know that God will always come through for us. I am a testimony of his answers. Whatever the outcome of things I had gone through, I realized that it was God who, at the precise moment I was about to give up (And I had thought of giving up many times!) God always came through for me.

Still on having faith in God, the Bible narrated the story of Moses who did not see himself as the man God could use to carry out the task that God had set before him. However, he had faith and through it, he allowed God to use him to lead the Israelites out of their captivity in Egypt. Even when the Israelites groaned and cursed God on the way out of Egypt, Moses looked up to God until he kept his promises in the end.

Notice that God did not keep his promises to Abraham, to Moses, to David and to many other men and women in the Bible because they were perfect or worthy. In fact, most of them were people with a questionable and flawed character. But they had decided to listen to God's voice in their life and to do the things he wanted them to do. It was not like God made choices for them. No, he gave them the freedom to choose, and thankfully for them and their offspring (of which every believer, in Christ, is today) they made the

191

right choice. God kept his promises to these men and women because they believed in him. Simple!

Another story of faith is that of Joshua who trusted God and his word, leading to the fall of the walls of Jericho. When Moses was old and lay dying, when the Israelites were in need of a new leader amongst them, God called Joshua to the task. Instead of complaining that he was unworthy to fit into the feet of an extraordinary prophet like Moses, as most people would have done today, Joshua did not look at the feat that Moses accomplished during his lifetime. On the other hand, he surrendered to the will of God to help him lead his people into the Promised Land. Joshua consolidated some of the things Moses couldn't do when he was alive. Because he trusted God, the promises made to Moses became his:

"Every place that the sole of your feet will tread upon I have given to you, just as I have promises to Moses... No man shall be able to stand before you all the days of your life. Just as I was with Moses, so I will be with you. I will not leave you or forsake you" (Joshua 1:3; 5)

Did God keep his promises to Joshua? Yes! The Israelites were able to enter the Promised Land and many years later as Joshua lay dying at 110 years old, the Bible reported that he "sent every man to his inheritance" and he, too, "was buried in the land of his inheritance" (Joshua 24:28-29).

That is what having faith in God and following his will can do. Joshua was able to take over from Moses the leadership of revolting former slaves who had nothing to call their own to inheritance!

What about Gideon? His faith in God saw him conquered the Midianite army with just a small of army of three hundred men.

You have heard the above stories several times. I brought them here to let you know that faith in God can allow you to overcome any obstacle that comes before you. Pray daily, conform to God, build a relationship with him and see him love and bless you right back! He is your father. Draw close to him. Allow the Holy Spirit to lead you and guide you daily. He will show you how to do that thing you've always wanted to do better!

Learn a lesson from what it means to be a disciple and be one yourself. Be humble. You are not perfect. You know far less than you think you know. Follow God, the source of all knowledge, and listen to his voice daily telling you what to do to arrive at the right place of your dreams. I have discovered that each time I strive to hear God's voice first before doing anything, whether that thing has to do with me, my husband, or my children, I always do it better. God is a rewarding

God. But he only rewards those who are called into obedience.

The entirety of my life has made me a true witness of God's favor that is capable of turning everything around.

Even though I went to prison and was a convicted of a felony, I am proud to say today that my record has been wiped clean!

Even though I was in and out of mental institutions, I am proud to say I have not had to see a psychiatrist or take medications in over two years!

Even though I had lost my children to the system temporarily, I am proud to say that they are all with me today!

Even though, I had lost my mother at a young age, I am proud to say that God sent me a God mother and a grandmother to love me unconditionally. My grandmother won her battle

195

with cancer and went on to be with the Lord. But I'm grateful that she was able to see me saved and living a life pleasing to God before her passing.

Even though I went through some emotionally and physically abusive relationships that should have left me a mess, I am proud to say that God sent me a husband that treats me like a Queen. Today, a lot of people see me and wonder how I went from that to this and my response is always: MY FAITH IN GOD! In him, I have found a friend to tell all my problems to and he never leads me in the wrong direction.

To the faithful one who loses, God has a way of giving you back double for your trouble.

I want to leave this with you today. We are all on a journey. Let go of the wheel and let God drive for you. When we grab the wheel of our lives and try to turn things around on our own, we are assured of nothing, but a life filled with wreckage.

We will be unsuccessful every time we try. God specializes in turning things around even though we don't know how to do it. Your situation may look impossible as mine did so many times and may even seem as if there isn't much hope for change. Before you allow the enemy to discourage you, remember that God's capable hands are on the steering wheel turning things around for you. He is moving you out of the storm you are currently in and taking you to a place of peaceful, joyous, and victorious living. The Lord is working in your favor right now as you read this. There is nothing too hard for him to do:

"Behold I am doing a new thing now it springs forth do you not perceive it? I will make a way in the wilderness and rivers in the desert" (Isaiah 43:19).

The "new thing" is what I had to get an understanding of myself. This was a wilderness promise! In that one scripture, God tells them that he will make a way in the wilderness and rivers in the desert. This encouragement was tailor-made for the dry, barren wilderness season. Right in the place of hopelessness is where God chooses to make his promise of a turnaround. I know you probably don't understand why you even have to go through the wilderness, but this dry place was necessary. This is where God chooses to perform his greatest work in your life.

Do not be discouraged. You can be saved. You can be happy. You can have the life you've always dreamed of. It doesn't matter what you did before. You have read my story to the end. I have survived, haven't I?

Yes! I Survived and So Will You!

www.ingramcontent.com/pod-product-compliance
Lightning Source LLC
Chambersburg PA
CBHW072002090426
42740CB00011B/2049